Interpretation Second

Interpretation Second

Understanding Human Creation

Paul Tarsleh

Paul Tarsleh
Interpretation Second

Published by Spines

ISBN: 979-8-89569-715-3

Like He did in Heavens, God has been dealing with the earth in dispensations.

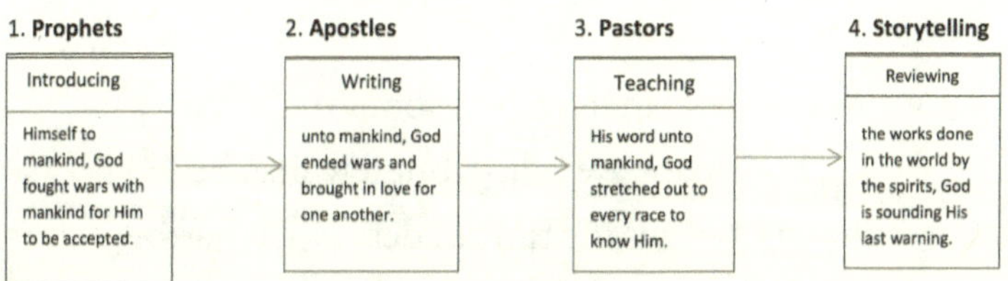

- **Time for teaching how to be righteous is over; it's quizzing and review time.**
  Remember that before a final exam in school, a teacher gives a quiz and a review. So, this is God's own time to quiz on what has been taught and review all that has been written. And before court action takes place, sometimes a judge gives legal advice, so this is God's own time to give His final advice.

- In this review, there are two Spiritual Truths that remain the secret things of the new world to come. God chooses to be silent on them due to some peculiar reasons.

- In this review, there is only one place previously chosen by God to be the peace center for all peoples to run to, to learn peace, but the people there have neglected peace talks and have lost their purpose in the world. God wants to defend Himself against some misunderstandings of His actions to them right now before the world. Therefore, let the world open its ears.

- Every Christian has heard about the narrow gate and how many are called, but few shall be chosen. Now is the time to define that narrow gate and how few shall be qualified among the many who're doing the work of God today.

- Every man knows how sweet the fish is, but not all know whether human poop makes the fish sweeter. This you'll know only when you open the fish's gut after it has just eaten poop. This is how the sweet things we do are made of poop [dirty things], but we don't see how dirty until now when God opens up the guts of our lives.

- Before the first world was destroyed, Noah was sent to advance God's warning. Now, I am that physical man to offer God's warning to physical men.

- Oh! See how pitiful it is to be rich and later turn poor; it's just how the world majority goes about enjoying the world in all of its riches [everything that glitters to the majority here in this world and they do every day], but the same way a majority of people shall suffer perpetual gnashing and grunting in heavenly prison while a very tiny number [like the few suffering on earth to do things right] shall rest in heavenly paradise.

These issues in this mission statement are brought to the people of the world in four major books, and this is just one of them.

Contents

Part Two

Part Three

Preface

Having acquired vast knowledge of the deep, I (Paul Tarsleh) from the theocratic school of the Highest Spirit, God, have come to reveal the Spirit's hidden secrets.

I had already been deprived of attending a Bible school in 2006, when I decided to pursue a two-year Evangelical Ministry Study at the "Maranatha Evangelical School" of the Liberian Refugee's Assembly of God Church in Tabou, Ivory Coast. So, whatever I say is not of any man but of the Spirit directly.

My Spiritual knowledge was acquired after a mysterious lifting of my body from bed on the night I returned home from the first day of Bible school, which ended that same day. That lifting, which triggered Christ down to earth into my body, was the beginning of what we're about to benefit from today through all the information in this book.

The Spirit put me in a Spiritual school, and at some

point in my spiritual training sessions, the Spirit told me that through the wicked ones, I was deprived of receiving the word of God. The spirit said since I was earlier deprived of studying the Bible, it was good for me to first receive the word of God directly from the Spirit before I could work with religious people for the scripture-to-scripture references concerning all that I was about to hear.

However, many people he met earlier questioned the authenticity of his revelations from God in this modern age full of false teachers, but Apostle Abraham Joe Kiamue made the difference. He agreed to collaborate with the Theocratic ministry, reviewed this book, and gave his endorsement. The author can't stop half to be thankful enough to him and his church.

Earlier, this lack of endorsement from people slowed down the success of this work and led him to replicate this book in 2024. Getting this book and the other three republished cost him a financial setback.

Another way he got scriptural references and cited good examples of biblical events was during a 2018 Saturday Bible study in Sacramento, California, U.S.A., with a Jehovah's Witnesses member named Nickolas, who helped him make the necessary corrections to those errors he had in his first publication in 2013 concerning the creation of every human race.

Nickolas told him that there was some black color reference in the story of Noah after the Flood concerning the nations' making. That single statement led Paul to search Noah's story, and he discovered that "Ham," Noah's son, is said to have been darker than his other two brothers. Thus, he established what people regard today as a biblical basis for how black Africans came to be.

Thanks to Nickolas, PAUL discovered Noah's darker son, Ham, which helped him see behind the Jewish assertion of black origin.

But this didn't change the story about how heavenly science created man in three major peoples [Fair {**White**}, Dusky {**Semi-White**} and Dark/**Black**]; each group of distinct humankind has its internal divisions in physical look, speech, coloration, and intelligence.

Introduction

May I invite you to join me as we search for the missing history sections and investigate the unknown?

This book is the full story of human creation but focuses on black origin.

Early in January 2018, the President of a great nation defamed black people with ridiculous name-calling, while in Israel, Africans were also labeled as having "Cancer and AIDS virus" and needed to be burned.

But before the black race was vehemently defamed, this book was already in draft and would explore several topics related to blackness. It would also explore all we need to know about human origin, both Spiritually and physically.

The organic purpose of this book is to stretch out the Bible (open the inner linings of the biblical accounts provided early on in human creation) by revealing the truth about how the clean color (white), half-clean color (semi-white), and dark color (black) were all made even though the Bible appeared to have depicted only one color of mankind for both Adam and Eve. That is, the Bible ("*Bibleur*" meaning "Two Worlds") said only two persons – Adam and Eve – were created in the beginning, but the same Bible didn't make any indication of whether one of them was black.

The depictions in the Bible without different human colors raise questions about which color God made first and how or when other colors came about.

While the biblical story of Ham says he was the darker one of the three sons of Noah, there seems to have been an assumption on how black color (black race) came into this world, which is why this book puts it differently, starting with a question on why mankind, particularly Ethiopians, have stopped changing forms (metamorphosing) if, at all, there is any truth in the metamorphosis of any ancient human among the first dark color of the Asiatic people. This calls into question whether [indeed] the darker Asians could change form into the dark/black color now found in Africa, precisely below the northern part of Africa.

Obviously, **Ham** was not black but dark; he became associated with black skin through folk etymology, as this book proves in the forthgoing.

Even before this book gives a new version in Part II under a subtitle *forming of physical man* on how black race was made, it reveals that pigmentation is a Spiritual make that occurs within every tribe and every race and that those of Cush (taken to be Ethiopians) whom the Bible referenced to be descendants of Ham are of no exception. As a people, they also have different pigmentations in skin color and eye color, including differences in height and size.

Before going any further with this black story, people first need to know that Abraham originated from a village called Ur, located in the Mesopotamia region. Because Abraham came from Noah's lineage, it's easy to understand that Ham is a son of an area called Mesopotamia. So, the variation in the skin color of Noah's three sons - Japheth (fair), Shem (dusky), and Ham (darker), did set the beginning of pigmentation in skin color for the people of Mesopotamia. This further means that Ham's dark skin group is still a part of the people of Mesopotamia who have never changed and couldn't change forms even now any time they bear children.

Cognizant of the fact that renowned religious people might argue that the people of Cush are the same who metamorphosed into the kind of blacks that are spread all over East, Central, West, and South Africa, this book says that the dark people of Ethiopia we see today are the same kind of Asiatic group of people who can be found in North Africa who are neither charred black nor sparkling white. They, too, have never changed color, neither will they ever do.

My inspiration reveals that at the time, the people of Asia, among whom Ham is mentioned in the book of Genesis, were multiplying and traveling in all directions; the black man was living on the other side of the world.

The presence of another humankind (the dark/black people) living on the other side of the world blocked the spread of the migrant Asiatic group from moving down the land now called Africa. Instead of continuing to migrate down the jungles, they spread through the northern part of the continent, expanding through other countries today, such as Egypt, Tunisia, Algeria, Libya, and Morrocco.

One lead we have is a striking Bible story that describes the river called "Gihon," which is said to encompass (encircle) Cush, Gen. 2:10-14 KJV. The Gihon River is one of the four biblical rivers depicted in the Garden of Eden. These rivers are in the Mesopotamia region in Asia. Is it not better to say that Cush is in Mesopotamia, where the Gihon River encircles it?

From the Bible, we learn that Ham's descendants lived in Cush. I believe that when Bible writers in those days found some dark Asiatic people living in the Kingdom of Gojjam, now Ethiopia in Africa, they were forced to assume that the Asiatic Gojjam people were the same people who had changed into a completely new breed of humankind called the black people who now occupy the vast portion of Africa.

This belief of mine came about only after listening to the Storyteller [The Highest Spirit], who told me that the black race didn't come from the Ethiopian people and therefore urged me to ask theologians why present-day Ethiopians are not still bearing black children if at all there was any truth in what early Bible interpreters wrote. He was the one who told me that those early interpreters made some assumptions after gathering the scrolls that Moses left behind and were confused over how black people they met by the time of compiling their history into one book, now called the Bible, came about.

However, there is no problem calling the Kingdom of Gojjam "Cush" since it's also possible to find traces of the Asiatic people from what was supposed to be "Cush/Kush" crossing the Red Sea to the ancient "Kingdom of Gojjam" now called "Ethiopia" in Africa. This means that some Ethiopians are from the Middle East, while others are African indigenes.

Speaking of those from Asia to Cush/Ethiopia is equivalent to saying that Israelis today are also from another land called initially "Ur," then located in the ancient city of Mesopotamia. [The ruins of Ur are approximately midway between the modern town of Baghdâd, Iraq, and the head of the Persian Gulf, south of the Euphrates River, on the edge of the Al-Jarrah Desert. The site of Ur is known today as Tall al Muqayyar, Iraq.]

From the above description of the Gihon-Cush in Asia, it's good to say that during the compiling of Jewish history, the Jews wrongly took the dark Asians who lived in Gojjam in Africa, at the time, to be the reason for seeing Cush/Kush in Africa instead of seeing it in Asia. Probably for the same purpose of consistency to be a part of world history, the people of Gojjam used the Abay River (Blue Nile) to be the river that encircles the Cush to justify the Jewish assertion.

Let me break it down in question form: If the Bible story that describes the Garden of Eden as having four big rivers (Pishon, Gihon, Tigris, and Euphrates) is true that they are in Mesopotamia, then why is the area (Cush) surrounded by Gihon not found in the same Mesopotamia region? This question proves that the people of Gojjam (now Ethiopia) were also wrong to have taken the Blue Nile for Gihon, a tactical attempt to justify Gojjam as the biblical Cush.

Based on this misconception of people and places, this book reveals that the darker people of Cush/Kush lived in

Asia in the Mesopotamia area. They are just one dark Middle Eastern group that lives among other Middle Eastern colors, just as some dark-skinned Indians live among the different Asiatic Indian colors [Asiatic Indians who have a Capital City as "New Delhi"].

In my quest for details on the Gihon River, I came across an article from "Wikipedia, *Creative Commons Attribution-ShareAlike License,*" so I'll be glad to share an excerpt below:

Quote; "The author of Genesis describes Gihon as "encircling the entire land of Cush," a name associated with Ethiopia elsewhere in the Bible. This is the reason that Ethiopians have long identified the Gihon (*Giyon*) with the Abay River (Blue Nile), which encircles the former kingdom of Gojjam. From a geographic standpoint, this would seem impossible, since two other rivers said to issue out of Eden, the Tigris and the Euphrates, are in Mesopotamia", unquote.

In furtherance, I also learned that other scholars have long identified Cush as the ancient Kassite Kingdom, an area in Mesopotamia repeatedly flooded by the Tigris and Euphrates rivers.

One of the world's famous philosophers, Herodotus, supported the idea that there were two Cushes: one African Ethiopia and another northern Asiatic Ethiopia.

As the author of this book, I agree that Herodotus's assertion is very correct. I urge Bible readers to accept that there was an Asiatic Cush/Kush whose people traveled across the Red Sea to settle down at the place now called "Ethiopia" in Africa, which brought about the belief of Cush in Africa.

And in my personal view, having read scientific theory about continental drift [the breaking up of the earth's crust into large pieces of lands divided and surrounded by waters], the stretch of land from Egypt down to Ethiopia may have been part of Middle Eastern habitat before the continental drift that caused a body of water (Red Sea) to form between middle eastern nations and African nations. In fact, Egypt in Africa is connected to Jordan in the Middle East by land, except that an artificial waterway called the "Suez Canal" was built between the two countries to connect the Red Sea to the Mediterranean Sea in 1869 (1859-1869.)

This means that when those who compiled the stories in Genesis saw dark people in Africa, they may not have been wrong about being the people of Cush in the Middle East since that piece of land may have previously been in Asia before the continental drift. Still, they were equally wrong to have concluded that the migrants were the ancestors of the charred black people of Africa because these same kinds of dark people in Ethiopia share the same sort of physical identity as those of Asia.

The Spirit told me that those Arab migrants have never changed, but if they had indeed changed before, THEN their offspring today must be able to continue to bear black children even in modern times.

Obviously, some modern Ethiopians are direct children of the ancient Gojjam Kingdom, and there has never been any genocide to wipe them all off the face of the earth. So, the absence of any report of genocide in the Gojjam Kingdom validates why they should still be having black children as their ancestors did, according to biblical assertion.

To this end, I must emphasize that no race has ever

changed into another human species since creation; not even intermarriage has ever produced a totally new race.

However, currently, there are reports of some white or black or other couples giving birth to babies that are entirely different from them. That's why I inquired from the Spirit World this morning, September 20, 2024@8:23 AM, and I got an answer. I was told that such crossbreeding is happening from the side of good spirits to bring about peace among racially divided communities of the one human world. It is to make people see themselves as one people of God without looking down on others because of their colors.

Above all else, one of the primary concerns of this book is that we should know that the Bible was written in short terms (Parables) without providing all the details on everything.

One of the shortest ways the Bible was inspired is demonstrated by any statement that says, "And God said, let there be... and it was so." Such short statements in the Bible represent God's revelation of technology (the fastest way to make things) that existed in Heaven, while the earth did not yet know technology when the word of God was written.

The statement that God just spoke, and the system of things came about instantly, is a parable of the wise one (God) saying to mankind that everything He did was done very fast as opposed to the length of time people of Bible days took to do things.

Can you imagine that any piece of artwork [let's say making of a machete] that took several hours or days to pass through the fire of a blacksmith who used bellows to blow fire in those ancient days can now take just a few minutes to make in our modern-day factories due to technology? So, what language can modern men use to speak of their jobs?

So, the lack of these details in the Bible shows the shortage of several emphases the Bible should have provided for us to know what specific part other people played in the creation of things for which the pronoun "us" appeared in the Bible: "And God said, let **us** make man in our image, after our likeness..." (Gen. 1:26 KJV)

Considering the use of the plural pronoun, *us* means that God gave commands to other people called "angels" who existed with Him in Heaven, and they worked harder in the creation of things.

The angels may [scientifically] be compared to robots we command or use today in our time to do things faster than human beings do.

So, the involvement of other people (angels) also means that there were processes of heavenly creations by these angels, who have been God's robots to do the things required to create everything.

The absence of details further evades the sense that the earth and everything in it were just made at the snap of God's finger. Oh yes, even as fast as technology is, every bit of work still requires time to start and finish. This means that each piece of creation done by God took time, resources, and people who worked hard in Heaven to have it done for God.

Sadly enough, the lack of details on heavenly creation has become the reason why we do not know how three primary human colors [the **White man** {clean color – European, Japanese, Chinese with their likes, Russian, etc}, the **Semi-White man** {half-clean color – Jew/Arab, Pakistani, Asiatic

Indian, north American Indian, Mexican, Brazilian, and Porto Rican with their likes}, and **Black man** {dark color of Africa}] were made very distinctly.

Once again, the lack of in-depth details on heavenly creations served as a basis for why the Bible didn't say that the kind of black people who currently inhabit Africa did or didn't exist in the First World before the Flood. Instead, it says that the black man evolved from the dark Ham who lived in the First World and survived the Flood to start the Second World with his father and siblings.

This assertion made by early interpreters of God's word in Genesis showed the strife they carried on in their days to give meanings to the scripts Moses left behind and is rather unfortunate to say Noah's son, Ham, who bore all the characteristics of present-day Arabic man, had metamorphosed into an entirely new kind of human being now called "Black African" [Also known as Negro in America].

As we conclude, this book has three major parts [Part One, Part Two, and Part Three], each with its subdivisions: headings.

The first part contains spiritual events in which the secret things of human creation are simplified.

The second part compares the black race to other races. It contains political, economic, and historical events of all races. It contrasts and compares white man's achievements to black man's achievements since creation, even while we all are imbued with corrupt minds.

The third part focuses on the underdevelopment issues in Africa.

And hey, this book combines three major events about

mankind—his Spiritual existence, his culmination into physicality, and his distinctive features of racial colors.

Finally, let me quickly awaken you to the fact that this book is far from conventional storytelling because it contains some Spiritual words with unique meanings, unlike how people have conventionally taken these exact words. For example, in this book and all of my other books, the word Heavens has spelled four different ways: (1) *Heavens-* always plural in spelling, which will always refer to all the spheres of the milky air taken together with God's Throne for any discussion, (2) *Heaven-*which has capital 'H' but in singular denotes that only God's Throne [His Sphere] is in the writer's mind to discuss, (3) *heavens-* is excluding God's Throne [Upper Heaven] from the discussion of all the lower heavens (spheres) in which the angels of God conduct heavenly activities, and (4) *heaven-* is indicating that just one heaven (one sphere) of the lower spheres is being considered in mind by the author.

Similarly, you may sometimes encounter two different spellings for one word, such as "Spirit" and "spirit," which can mean God Himself as Spirit under discussion and God's lower spirit [messenger] in the writer's mind.

Likewise, you may come across some new words that God has put on my tongue, such as the word "Bibleur," meaning "two worlds," which comes to us as the Spiritual word for the word "Bible."

Because of these strange things about this book, conventionality should be less relevant to understanding certain parts of it.

Part One

Reports from another world

Where Did We Come From?

The Christian community hasn't understood the Book of Genesis until now. There have been debates among Christian denominations about the Spiritual existence of man. I haven't found any denomination coming so close to what the Spirit of God revealed to me in 2008 concerning the pre-existence of humans before turning into physicality, except the Latter-day Saints church.

What does the LDS church say?

Sunday, May 5th, 2019@7:10 A.M. While I was awaiting a US Work Permit to find a job to raise money to publish the books God has inspired me to write, I came across the topic **"Where did I come from?"** in a Bible teaching Tract from the Latter Days Saints (LDS) Church. The topic *"Where did I come from?"* is on page 2 of the Tract titled *"The Plan of*

Salvation." It is written therein, "Your life didn't begin at birth, nor will it end at death. You are made up of a spirit body (sometimes called the soul) and a physical body. Your Heavenly Father created your spirit, and you lived with Him as a spirit before you were born on earth. You knew and loved Him, and He knew and loved you. This period is called pre-earth life".

Oh my gosh, see what the Spirit has given unto a man among modern people in God's continuous strive to enlighten mankind on the things written centuries ago in the Book of Genesis but were never understood by those who gathered Moses' works and compiled them into what the Church has with them.

I do love the report, and I take it essential today because it lays the foundation of what has been fully disclosed to me, another modern man nicknamed "the interpreter, or story-teller, or revelator," who has the duty to explain to all the peoples of the earth everything hidden secret of the Spirit world.

Even some of these things were revealed by those who came before the storyteller, but they were never explained better by the early people since they were not given the power of interpretation.

Therefore, God told me (the storyteller) in 2008 that all the things that I was taught [in the school of the Spirit of God] during the period expanding over two years (2006-mid 2008) have all been written about by the people who came before me. Still, their works contained some lapses (gaps) that He [God] has come to correct and fill.

Therefore, on the things of man's Spiritual existence, God brought forth to me Ezekiel 28:13-17 to begin the history of Satan's existence in the Garden of Eden, where he (Satan) did wrong things by taking God's position to deceive man before he [Satan] was thrown down to the earth.

The essentiality of the Garden in establishing the truth about man's pre-existence can not be understated as we begin this journey of a new day.

So, the spirits of God started giving me the details on this Spiritual Man by first starting with Lucifer [now Satan] in the Garden of Eden and his interaction with man there.

They, the many spirits that came down on earth to me one after another as lecturers on various issues, said to me that everything about today's mission [review or go all over the Bible] hangs entirely on man's ability to get the full understanding of the Garden of Eden, which is the place of many activities at the beginning of man's existence.

Why has the Bible been chosen among many books in particular? The answer is that the Bible is the oldest piece of human work mysteriously dictated by a supernatural being called "God," a word that stands for "**Go d**emonstrate" or "**Go** out to **d**emonstrate."

One thing to note is that His wisdom in writing has never always been understood unless a special interpretation is given to a special person. This has been the case due to the high level of figures of speech used in telling heavenly tales.

One such figure of speech God used so cleverly is *allegory*. It is His secret way of using something as a symbol (icon) to represent something else. Let's say allegory is God's wisest way of talking about something when He actually means another thing.

Allegory is common in our everyday dreams when we see a strange or familiar creature running behind us or, worse, devouring us. Still, when we wake up on the other side of the two worlds (Spiritual and Physical), we see something different befalling us [the opposite of what we encountered in the Spiritual world]. It all depends on the degree of the Spiritual attack (the dream) that determines how dangerous our encounter with other people or things on this physical side could be.

So, let me give an example of how dreams work with me. I want to cite one that enticed me. [Dream] In 2021, I was looking down over the sea atop a hill. I saw a big fish come close to the shore. I hurried down the cliff to grab it, but as I came close, I saw it going back into the deep. My heart panted, and I began to clamp back the cliff. It was exhausting because there were many twists and turns on the hill. [Wake life] Two days later, I received a letter from the President of Penguin Random House, a renowned traditional publishing firm, telling me that they had seen my book titled **Oh, Tarapul** [republished twice as *Tarapul, Oh*, and now *The Book of Interpretation Fourth*]. The letter conveyed their interest in my book, but they said I was not promoting it and didn't have sales, so I should do something to increase my chances of them picking it for a book deal. [How could it be connected to the dream?] When I sent the letter to my publishing company (IUniverse) to confirm its authenticity, they said yes, it came from Penguin Random House. They said they could help me promote the book, but the hitch was the cost for them to promote the book for me was too high. Instead, I opted for a low-price service with some guys who said they were running a book marketing firm (InkedPub Ltd, Hudson House, 8 Albany St., Edinburgh, EH1 3QB www.inkedpubltd.com) and could help me out, but they ended up being scammers. So, I lost over USD 5,000.00 to them [details can be a different story]. Thus, I saw that the big fish represented the big traditional firm [allegory], my burning desire for them represented the same desire for the fish [allegory], my attempt to promote the book was my attempt for the fish [allegory], and my failure to succeed in the book promotion process was my failure to grab the fish [allegory].

So, you see how far apart the two events in the two worlds are? They show how opposite the Spiritual works with the physical. That's how powerful allegory is.

In the case of the Garden of Eden, now under microscopic study, allegory is that figure of speech that tells us how our world is a replica (a copy of the Spiritual world), such that everything, including ourselves-humans and every name on earth, has been duplicated after Spiritual existences. This means that what we call the earth and everything that is in it has a model in the hands of God in Heaven, and God called it His architectural design.

Unfortunately, the people who picked up the pieces of writing that Moses left behind were perplexed by what he (Moses) drew as the Garden of Eden, in which God gave names to the people, places, rivers, objects, and minerals, which would be repeated/duplicated in the physical.

However, those misunderstandings happened because

the early interpreters had already known similar names and places on earth, so it was easy to say that the Garden of God was on earth.

Even when the book of Ezekiel was written several hundred years after Genesis, the people still didn't recognize what God brought out for them to understand.

This misunderstanding of God's word has lived on from the old to the present, and the people say there is nothing wrong with it. But God says it matters, so He has brought a retelling of the old stories.

He started with the telling of the story about the beginning of all beginnings that includes everything about Lucifer (now Satan), and this is where the book of Ezekiel 28:13-17 makes us understand that Satan was one of the angels that learned (trained) in the Garden but was thrown down to the earth when Jehovah found waywardness in Him. It reads, v 13: Thou has been in **Eden the Garden of God**; every precious stone was thy covering, the sardius, topaz, and the diamond, the beryl, the onyx, and the jasper, the sapphire, the emerald, and the carbuncle, and gold: the **workmanship** of thy tabrets and of thy pipes was prepared in thee in the day that thou was created. (v 14) Thou art the anointed cherub that covereth; and have set thee so: thou wast upon the holy mountain of God; thou hast walked up and down in the midst of the stones of fire. (15) Thou wast perfect in thy ways from the day that thou wast created, till iniquity was found in thee. (16) By the multitude of thy merchandise [knowledge as a good] they have filled the midst of thee with violence, and thou hast sinned: Therefore, I will cast thee as profane out of the mountain of God: and I will destroy thee, O covering cherub, from the midst of the stones of fire. (17) Thine heart was lifted up because of thy beauty, thou hast corrupted thy wisdom by reason of thy brightness: I will **cast thee to the ground**, I will lay thee before Kings, that they may behold thee. (This is KJV, but the NIV says, "So I threw you to the earth.")

Still, there are other scriptures making other indications. In Revelation 12:7-9, Satan is said to have been hurled down, hurled to the earth when war broke out in Heaven, and He and His collaborators lost their place: (v 7), And there was **war in heaven**: Michael and His angels fought against the dragon; and the dragon fought and his angels. (8) And prevailed not; neither was their place found any more in **heaven**. (9) And the great dragon was cast out, that old serpent, called the Devil, and Satan, which deceiveth the whole world: He was **cast out into the earth,** and His angels were cast out with Him. (This is KJV, but NIV says, "hurled down, hurled to the earth.")

Most strikingly, in Revelation 12:12, Jehovah is said to have lamented (had pity) over the earth and adored (Praised/Blessed) the Heavens, saying that Satan has left the Heavens and gone down to the people of the earth and the sea. It reads: "Therefore rejoice, ye **heavens,** and ye that dwell in them. Woe to the inhabitants of the **earth** and of the sea! for the **devil is come down unto you**, having great wrath, because He knoweth that He hath but a short time."

Conclusive Facts

The book of Ezekiel clearly tells us that Satan was in the Garden, from where He was thrown down. Then, the book of Revelation tells us that the war was fought in Heaven, and Satan lost his ground there and was hurled down. The same Revelation also clearly distinguishes between Heaven and earth, saying that Heaven should rejoice for being freed of Satan, but the earth should cry for being occupied with Satan.

Let's depict this scenario.

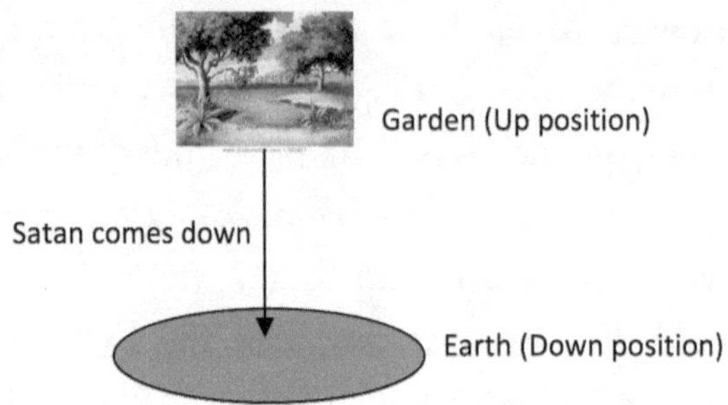

Then there is this saying about the 'Tree of Life' that has constantly been watched over by the angels of God, so that man would not take from it and be wise also like God and His angels, which reads in Genesis 3:24, NIV: "After he drove the man out, he placed on the east side of the Garden of Eden cherubim and a flaming sword flashing back and forth to guard the way to the tree of life." ... Genesis 3:24, NLT: "After sending them out, the LORD God stationed mighty cherubim to the east of the Garden of Eden."

Let's not forget that this Tree of Life exists with the Tree of Knowledge in the Garden (Genesis 2:9). And let's note that angels are Spiritual beings who live only in the Spirit Realm, so whatever they do surely happens in the Spirit Realm.

In the New Testament, Luke 10:18 also contains the word 'Fall', which Jesus used to tell His disciples that He (Jesus) was at the beginning (Heaven) and saw what happened to Satan when he (Satan) was defeated.

Because of all the above, it's now more straightforward for us to reason together that Lucifer couldn't have been on earth (standing on the ground) and at the same time fell to the same earth after he was thrown out of Heaven. So, whatever the reasons that the people of old thought the Garden was on earth, remains the primary thing to find out from this book.

Therefore, I bring you the news that the 'Tree of Life' still exists in the Spirit Realm, where the angels of God live to keep the way of the Tree from another touch.

Here is what God said in Genesis 3:22: "And the Lord God said, behold, the man is become as one of us, to know good and evil: and now, lest he put forth his hand, and also take of the Tree of Life, and eat, and live forever." [This is KJV, but NIV says, "He must not be allowed to take also from the Tree of Life."]

This was a new order that God gave in Heaven after the other Tree (the Tree of Knowledge of Good and Evil) in the Garden was violated.

Isn't it wonderful that God warned the angels (even Satan) not to allow man to touch the Tree of Life?

If you ask me (PAUL, the interpreter), I'll say that the Tree of Life could be the actual thing called "Life," which every living thing needs to continue to exist. So, in my opinion, the reason that God refused to let man take hold of it could be the same reason why human science is still struggling to put life in robots to make a complete human being without waiting for natural birth.

God and Satan working in the Garden

There are two major reasons why we have the Bible (*Bibleur*). One is to know about God, who made us, while the other is to know about Satan, whose attitude towards God brought about the separation between God and us.

Having said so, I want to quickly dismiss every notion of why any man would not like to hear about Satan because, without Satan, the coming of Jesus would have almost been useless. Without him, the world would have been as perfect as God wanted it to be. Without him, we (humankind) would have had no suffering in the world. And without him, the teaching of the Bible would have had no significance in the world.

Yes, because without Satan's rebellion, mankind would still be experiencing the walk around (visitation) of the Almighty God during any of His spare times. Also, without him, there wouldn't have been sins (wrongdoings) in this world.

So, you see, God created man and put him in a nursery [a Spiritual place of growing things before transplanting them into physicality] to develop well before He took them (man, the plants, animals, and minerals) to their actual destination. While they were still developing/growing, Lucifer came to the man and told him to do what it takes to become like them (God and the angels), to be wise, and to make clothes for themselves since they were nude/naked.

Therefore, Lucifer's action upset God, who told them to leave to live alone. This is what brought us here, here away from God, here away from the right things, where we're suffering under Satan's domination of our lives.

Did Satan really lie to Adam and Eve?

I think it's self-deceptive to say that discussing Satan is wrong. I think it's necessary because Satan is just one arm of God that possesses almost all the qualities that God Himself has, but he [Satan] is now misapplying those qualities in our world today.

His misapplication of God's power may have placed him on the wrong side, but it doesn't necessarily take him off the discussion about God.

Of course, teaching or discussing Satan's bad things should not be seen as exalting Satan because discussing biblical events with all its characters, including Satan, is just as important as discussing all world events with every country's leadership, whether good or bad. Thus, any attempt to leave one president's account out makes the country's history incomplete.

So, let's see what God and Satan did in Heaven.

In Gen. 2:9, God created two Trees (the Tree of Life and the Tree of Knowledge), and they were both good and important.

[let's maintain Satan's first name until he rebels] Lucifer knew the importance of the two trees, so in Gen. 3:4–5, he came to teach man the Importance of the Tree of Knowledge. NIV: [4] "You will not certainly die," the serpent said to the woman; [5] "For God knows that when you eat from it your eyes will be opened, and you will be like God, knowing good and evil."

Unfortunately, theologians think that to say Satan said the truth is to exalt Satan. Still, NO, it's not exaltation but rather stating the fact in the word of God by saying that Lucifer took authority into his own hands to apply the knowledge he received from God.

Satan's attitude is like a child telling his/her friends that his/her father has something hidden somewhere, then taking the friends to the place even with the knowledge of how wrong it is to do so.

So, let's find out how true Satan's statement is/was.

He said the woman's eyes shall be opened, and she shall be as wise as they (God & angels) are. So, when Eve heeded him, her [Their] eyes opened right after eating from the Tree of Knowledge, and she [They - Adam & Eve] realized how different she/they were from Lucifer, who wore beautiful garments. Let's see this in Gen. 3:7: "And the ***eyes of them both were opened, and they knew that they were naked***, [Now, go to the last line and see their wisdom after eating], and ***they sewed fig leaves together, and made themselves aprons.***"

Here, in Genesis 3:7, we now see the theology of how man started to make things for himself. This is a hidden theology that no man has ever preached in this word because Bible teachers think that it's to allude to Satan's scientific knowledge. Here, this theology reveals that Satan was the first to have taught man how to do things for himself. But, as wrong as his act was because it was prematurely done and not in his purview, the truth cannot be changed.

And, because Satan had already given them knowledge of science, which was due unto them [Adam & Eve] but to be given at the right time God had set in place, He (God) [reluctantly] fulfilled them later, as in Gen. 3:21 which reads: "Unto Adam also and to his wife did the Lord God make coats of skins, and clothed them."

Here, it can be inferred that God was reluctant to let man have this knowledge, as He warned the angels against teaching man how to use the Tree of Life, just as we read earlier in Gen. 3:22, which says, "And the Lord God said, behold, the man is become as one of us, to know good and evil: he must not be allowed to reach out his hand to take also of the Tree of Life, and eat and live forever."

So, both the defiant attitude of Lucifer and the disobedience of Adam & Eve led God to put them out of the Garden and place angels with swords around the Tree of Life to guard it every day.

From this point on, Lucifer's name changed to Satan, pronounced "Sat-an," meaning "Go against the laws" or "Turn against the laws." Also, from this point on, man (Adam and Eve) became the adopted children of Satan. This means that when God threw them (man and Lucifer) out of the Garden, which here is now explained as a particular part of the Heavens, they started to live with Satan in his Enclave, which was the new place he'd found in the outskirts of God's dwelling place.

So, what or where Heavens is?

I don't really know how most people define Heavens or what they think it looks like, but one thing that has been revealed to me is that Heavens is a plural word that stands for several layers (spheres) of the total mass of air hanging over this physical earth crust.

It may be spelled singularly as Heaven and heaven only when a writer intends to speak of a single layer, like when one thinks of the layer in which God resides (Heaven), which is often referred to as His Throne or another sphere (heaven) outside the Throne/Headquarters. The different spellings like Heaven, Heavens, heaven, and heavens came from this.

The whole story of man's existence

The book of Genesis is God's wisdom in telling the stories of how He designed the Heavens & the earth and the stories of how the physical world and its habitats came to be. The book is His story of architectural work, so there is one figure of speech amongst several that God used largely to write the book since it contains His layout plans of creations. This figure of speech is called '**Allegory**' that He used so well that the whole book appeared so real to physical man. He set characters in places so well that they all fit to be like physical things.

The way God created all that He made is just how man is doing now in this modern world of advanced science. It means man first crafts out a plan and puts all things in their places (architectural layout) before he may transform that plan into actual construction. See two models:

A

B

Royalty-free stock photo ID: 581197216 *Housing model – Images*

A) With technological means of designing, man is now capable to lay out a community with structures put in place like in this model, and it will seem real to a primitive village dweller.

B) Someone may take a photograph of a property and show it to another and say this his/her own property which could appear true to the other who has no other means to check the facts.

Inside this structure, a good designer may lay out how the seating capacity can be, even if it means to set human characters in the various seats.

What is God's actual architecture?

I mentioned to you earlier that everything on this earth is a replica of the Heavens. The following scriptures tell us that every knowledge man has comes from God. So, God's Architecture is the step-by-step way He created all things. Let's see what the Bible says about His Architecture:

Hebrews 3:4 says, "The builder of all things is God".

Hebrews 11:10b says, "Whose builder and maker is God".

[But "The Strongest NASB Exhaustive Concordance" -2000 Edition, page 80; interprets this verse the best way I received it, which says, "God is an Architect."]

Exodus 35:31 says, "And he hath filled him with the Spirit of God; in wisdom, in understanding, and in knowledge, and in all manner of workmanship." [The word 'Workmanship' here has been interpreted to me as being Art & Craft or Creational knowledge.]

KJV, Ezekiel 28:13 says, **"The workmanship of thy**

tabrets and of thy pipes was prepared in thee in the day that thou was created." [Full text: "[13]Thou has been in Eden the Garden of God; every precious stone was thy covering, the Sardius, topaz, and the diamond, the beryl, the onyx and the jasper, the sapphire, the emerald, and the carbuncle, and gold: the workmanship of thy tabrets and of thy pipes was prepared in thee in the day that thou was created.]

[Here, the word 'workmanship' clearly refers to the Scientific/Creational knowledge Jehovah gave Satan in the Garden of Eden.]

The above is ascribed to God, but man, being in God's image, can create, too. Below is man's way of creating things. So, let's see the pattern man follows when constructing a house.

Stage 1. **The Mental Construction (exploring/thinking):**

An architect first sits all by himself to think (mix things up in the brain) and build a picture of what should be constructed, how it should be constructed, and what needs to be placed in it with names.

This is called man's Dream/Vision/Plan to build.

1A. **Sketch:**

The architect makes a sketch (a rough drawing.)

1B. **Forecast:**

The architect makes detailed divisions into the parts of the construction design.

1C. **Blueprint:**

The architect makes a polished design of the whole as a finished design.

Stage 2. **The physical construction:**

The physical work is a structural work that starts with the casting of basement and laying foundation blocks with a material composition of sand, rocks, cement & steel... [as in the case of modern house construction.]

As we all know, according to his forecast, every architect builds a house part by part. He assigns time to each part and follows the time day by day- gathering, constructing, and destroying (breaking down some parts) simultaneously.

The physical construction is the last phase of the building. It is the real one, visible to every man's eye and touchable as well.

To demonstrate this architectural way of building, we decided to show two main photographs: one is an architectural drawing showing what looks like a physical object, while the other is a physical ongoing construction that has to go through many stages to become a finished one, as the final drawing is.

DEMONSTRATION ONE

A. Architectural Drawing for the kind of house a man wants to build.

In the picture above, a man keeps a mere drawing to express his dream, plan, or hope to construct a house like the drawing looks, but he has yet to actualize this vision into physicality.

DEMONSTRATION TWO

Let's say the man has begun to express
his vision into a physical construction
of what was expressed in a picture as a plan.

This construction work has to go through
its stages till it comes to a full
completion, similar to the demonstration one.

This means that God is the greatest Architect, not exceptional in constructing His Estates (the Heavens and the earth), including all that is in them. Also, considering Ezekiel 28:13- 17, the Garden was [is] a picture/model of the earth within the Heavens, which is why it was depicted with everything resembling the physical earth.

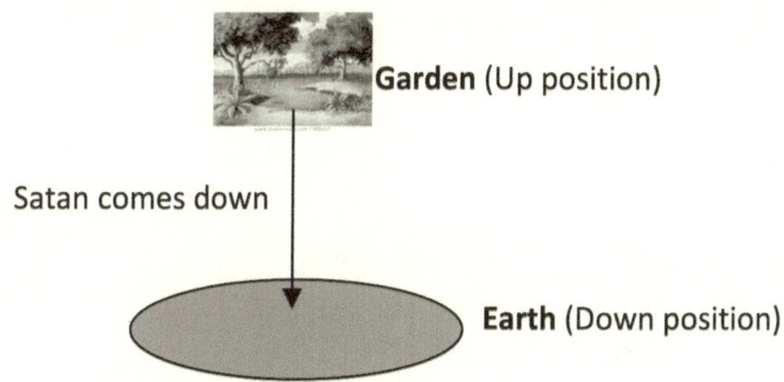

This further means that science was well advanced in the Heavens before the physical earth even started, and the 'Garden of Eden' then existed as one of the spheres of the Heavens. That's why it was shown to Moses [as in the depiction right above] while he was in a trance.

The earth has just started, as in DEMONSTRATION TWO far above, and is still going through its stages of construction through natural actions that break down hills and trees to make the earth level for human habitation.

This also means that the Garden was earlier shown as a completed earth, as in DEMONSTRATION ONE. Therefore, in God's architectural design, the Garden hosted the animals and the trees, with man as the caretaker.

Spiritual Existences

Let's repeat the Latter-Day Saints Church's version. While studying with them in Sacramento, California, USA, I came across the topic "*Where did I come from?*" on page 2 of their Bible teaching Tract, "*The Plan of Salvation.*"

Their version of spiritual man says: "Your life didn't begin at birth, nor will it end at death. You are made up of a spirit body (sometimes called the soul) and a physical body. Your Heavenly Father created your spirit, and you lived with Him as a spirit before you were born on earth. You knew and loved Him, and He knew and loved you. This period is called *pre-earth life*".

Hey, this report is vital today because it is the pillar of what God disclosed to me, the interpreter or storyteller, so I could explain to us how we lived in the Spirit Realm before culminating into physical beings. He said this report is right there in the Book of Genesis and the Book of Ezekiel, as well as other books, but early men didn't understand it from those books.

Therefore, God told me in 2008 that all the things that I was taught [in the school of the Spirit of God] from 2006 to mid-2008 have been written about by the people who came before me, but their works contained some lapses (gaps) that He [God] has come to correct and fill now during this review period.

Therefore, on the things of man's Spiritual existence, God brought forth to me Ezekiel 28:13-17 to open our eyes to the truth, beginning with Satan's existence in the Garden of Eden, where he (Satan) did wrong things by assuming God's authority but deceiving the Spiritual Man before he was thrown down to the earth.

So, they [the many Spirits that came to me one after another as lecturers on various issues] said everything about today's mission hangs entirely on man's ability to get the full understanding of the Garden of Eden since it is the place where all our troubles started from.

Juxtaposing Spiritual Existences

As stated early on, the Heavens is a real world, but it is the one that gave birth to this physical world. It first owned every name and event that this world of ours has [owns] now, which means that there are Spiritual existences that the Bible does contain that are as similar to what the earth contains. That's why God just told me that the people who collected the pieces of scrolls left behind by Moses and later compiled them into Jewish history that the whole world now celebrates as the Bible didn't fully understand that the figures depicted by Moses were just the symbols showing the names and places that God had already chosen in Heaven as the place to start His work among physical mankind.

But even after so many years of living with this wrong notion about the Spiritual earth (Garden of Eden), God revealed it to Ezekiel in the address to the King of Tyre. Yet the people of the Bible downplayed the significance of this portion of the book of Ezekiel only to hold on to the old perception of what the early people thought the Garden was. That's why God replayed the entire beginning of all beginnings to me, starting with the first verse in the Holy Bible.

Genesis 1:1

The spirits of God started playing a recording to me that says before a man begins to use his hands to make a particular kind of thing, he first sits all alone and thinks (explores) in his mind about all that he wants to do and how he wants to do it. I heard from the recording that this is the same way God first thought over everything that He wanted to do. Therefore, Genesis 1:1 says, "In the Beginning, God created the Heavens and the earth." [all translations should spell the word 'Heavens' in Genesis 1:1 with a capital H and an S because it is the root of all creations.] This was God's Mind. His Mind was to create several heavens [spheres] with all that should be in them and one earth with all that should be in it.

The story goes: Like a single cell containing several parts, God started as a single Force, becoming a Living Creature later. He swelled until He filled a space called the "Upper Heaven." From the first Heaven [Upper Heaven], He created the lower heaven [the Firmament, Gen. 1:6-8{as the first sphere before other spheres followed later}] and He created the earth (Gen'1:9-10), and they three became the one Force of God.

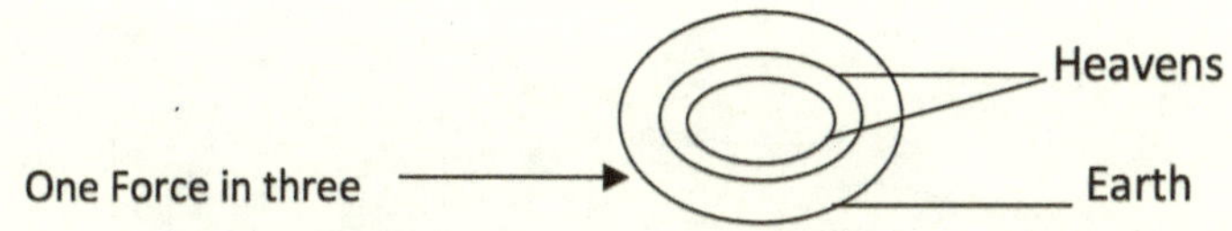

Genesis 1:2-10

> *This portion of the Bible is God's architectural forecast.*
> *When an architect has finished exploring*
> *in his mind, he sits down and makes a sketch*
> *with his drawing tools as a shadow of what*
> *is in the mind [this is called an architectural*
> *forecast].*
> *In a forecast, the architect shows out segments*
> *and their parts that make the whole.*

So, God began to bring forth His Mind by stretching/protruding downward of His Throne (one Cell that divides) into three, and the second heaven appeared (Genesis 1:6), and the earth appeared (Gen. 1:9.)

Protrusion of God's Spirit to the earth

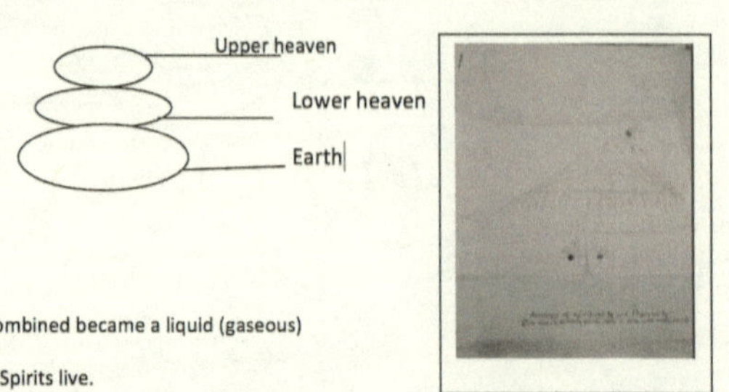

The two Heavens combined became a liquid (gaseous) World in which the Spirits live.

But the farther down He protruded, the better He curdled/thickened, and He became solid and hard to touch & hold by man [that's the earth's crust].

Remember, we told you earlier that all things on this physical earth are also present in the Spirit Realm, and all names given on earth have their roots in the Spirit Realm.

Therefore, every creation of God appeared more than once in the Bible. For example, you find water between the first Heaven (Gen. 1:1) and the second heaven (Gen. 1:6). You still find water between the second heaven and the earth (Gen. 1:9). Even so there is another water under the earth (Gen. 1:10). This is to give you the example of the sequences Spirituality (soft or unseen creations) followed till it culminated into Physicality (hard/touchable creations).

The separations in water indicate a fountain [origin] of water in the Heavens before a pool (collection) came on earth.

Please let me insert here that spirituality is a complex situation. It involves tangibles and intangibles. It is very similar to scientific inventions in that we can see and

> *touch our cell phones, but at the same time, we cannot see how messages are transmitted or received through them. This is why it is stupid enough to keep chasing behind what and how God did all that He did.*

Genesis 1:11-31

God's art of spiritual creation through segments became vivid here. In this portion, God made colorful designs of things in the Heavens and the earth. He gave them names and showed us their sequences/generations one after another.

So, in Gen.1:11, God began to deal with the earth alone as a segment. He brought forth the grass and tree kinds. He made them seeds and fruits.

In Gen.1:14-16 He dealt with the heaven alone and made it to host two lights – the greater & the lesser Lights being the Sun and the Moon. He also attached Satellites –the Stars (His own presence) with them.

In Gen.1:20-21, He took the Waters as a segment and made them host the fishes and the animals.

In Gen.1:24, He revisited the earth and made the animals according to their kinds, and He made Man in Gen.1:27.

> *These analogies can best be understood by factory workers who are involved in manufacturing processes.*

Those manufacturing vehicles know very well that to make a vehicle; you must do it part by part. Even as a part, you'll keep adding each part one by one.

Or if you are a carpenter, you'll know that to make a single bed; you must make it part by part and keep going to each part till you have done it whole.

That is to say, a carpenter may start a bed by making the legs first as a segment. In this case, the person cuts, plains, and varnishes the planks and then puts them. away for a while. So, after another time, the carpenter comes back to nail together the pieces that were let to dry off the varnish.

This is precisely what continued to happen when God was creating the Universe. Each time He made a segment and its parts, He revisited the same to add or finish with it. For this reason, the Bible put this adding and adding as, "And God said, And God said..."

Bible users surely learned that the human body is made of the Soul and the flesh, but they do not understand how this happened. For this reason, God has given me another analogy from human science.

Every moving object science has made is composed of two parts: the engine and the frame. Throughout science, you can see that the engine is the smallest part of the whole but, at the same time, is the most powerful component of the vehicle. The engine makes the model or make of the vehicle, and it cannot be altered, but the frame can be changed when anyone desires to do so.

Every Patent Right an inventor holds for a particular vehicle is for the engine.

Similarly, Jehovah God made two parts of the human being. This is why the Bible provides two different verses for the creation of man and two different verses for the creation of woman.

In Gen.1:27, God created [first] the two engines (Souls) of both the man and the woman, and this verse says: "So God created man in His own image, in the image of God created He him; male and female created He them." Like how different colors were made systematically [Races of human beings as explained later in this book], this creation of two genders incorporates how He (God) created both male and female together. Still, the scientific process [the unexplained part of God in the Jewish book] was done in succession, whereas the male was made first. He was called "son," which means "second" after the first image of God. The female followed and was called "daughter," which means "daughster-estiky" [it is a Spiritual word that describes a completely new creature/creation out of the second creation to do things that the son is not to do].

So, to talk about when man and woman were created, this verse [Gen.1:27] must have already completed the process, but because these two were just the engines that God had made, two other verses followed at two different times in the Bible. Therefore, in Gen.2:7, God created the frame of man, which says, "And the Lord God formed man of the dust of the ground, and breathed into his nostrils the breath of Life, and man became a living soul. [Please take note of the word 'Soul" God used because the frame covers the Soul, which is the engine that drives the human body.] Then God made the woman's frame, too, in Gen. 2:22, which also reads, "And the rib, which the Lord God had taken from man, made He a woman, and brought her unto the man." [Here, the female's soul has also been put in a frame called the woman's body.]

> *Is there something to grab here?*
> *Souls are not physical things. They live with God, and they are God's connectors or mediums used to get into physical things. They are compared to cables or wires through which electric powers are transmitted to any destination.*

Therefore, the man in Gen. 2:7 is still a Spiritual living thing with God, likewise the woman in Gen. 2:22.

But before the human bodies were formed out of the ground, these two living Souls, allegorized as "Adam" and "Eve," were placed in a nursery. This means they were placed somewhere God called the "Garden of Eden" to mature before they could be formed into the hard part from the ground of this hard earth [transferred to the hard ground].

How can we know that Adam & Eve are Spiritual Beings?

I, PAUL, do not personally know why theologians have blindly taught the Bible as a hundred percent physical human history when God has given scriptures for our understanding.

Firstly, God gave us scriptures that Satan existed in the Garden of Eden but was later thrown to the earth. Ezekiel 28:13 - 17) Thou has been in **Eden the Garden of God**; every precious stone was thy covering, the sardius, topaz, and the diamond, the beryl, the onyx, and the jasper, the sapphire, the emerald, and the carbuncle, and gold: the **workmanship** of thy tabrets and of thy pipes was prepared in thee in the day that thou was created. (:14) Thou art the anointed cherub that covereth; and have set thee so: thou wast upon the holy mountain of God; thou hast walked up and down in the midst of the stones of fire.

(:15) Thou wast perfect in thy ways from the day that

thou wast created, till iniquity was found in thee. (:16) By the multitude of thy merchandise they have filled the midst of thee with violence, and thou hast sinned: therefore, I will cast thee as profane out of the mountain of God: and I will destroy thee, O covering cherub, from the midst of the stones of fire. (:17) Thine heart was lifted up because of thy beauty, thou hast corrupted thy wisdom by reason of thy brightness: I will **cast thee to the ground**, I will lay thee before Kings, that they may behold thee. (This is KJV, but the NIV says, "**So I threw you to the earth.**")

Secondly, God said a war broke out in Heaven, and the Dragon (Satan) was brought down to the earth. Revelation 12:7 - 9) And there was **war in heaven**: Michael and His angels fought against the dragon; and the dragon fought and his angels. (:8) And prevailed not; neither was their place found any more in **heaven**. (:9) And the great dragon was cast out, that old serpent, called the Devil, and Satan, which deceiveth the whole world: He was **cast out into the earth**, and His angels were cast out with Him. (This is KJV, but another version says, "hurled down, hurled to the earth.")

Thirdly, God lamented over the earth that Satan had come down to it while He adored the Heavens, saying Satan had left it. Revelation 12:12: Therefore rejoice, ye **heavens**, and ye that dwell in them. Woe to the inhabitants of the **earth** and of the sea! for the **devil is come down unto you**, having great wrath, because He knoweth that He hath but a short time.

From these scriptures in the Bible, we learn that the Garden is above the ground and in the Heavens. Thus, those who lived in the Garden, beginning with Adam and Eve, should be understood as Spiritual human characters who have been duplicated to live on earth with hard bodies.

So, why would it be difficult for mankind to understand this book? Why would anyone continue arguing about the validity of the current work of the Spirit?

But what earth was Satan thrown down to?

Every church teaches Lucifer's fall to the earth, and it is said that he's moving around the world to deceive people. However, with all the news reports around the world, I had never heard of anyone spotting Satan (formerly Lucifer) anywhere in the world. No country hosts him anywhere in our big world. So, where is he? Why can't we see him?

Now is our opportunity to understand what the Bible calls the Earth.

The first thing to do is identify who he is. He is definitely a Spirit, and Spirits live in the Spirit world.

Therefore, the Earth Bible refers to the portion of Air hanging nearest to this physical earth. It is the spiritual Earth hosting the forces of nature responsible for holding the hard parts together. It is the air mass blowing our bodies, throwing down things, and containing every infection called a disease or virus.

Unfortunately, we cannot understand this entirely without understanding what Heaven is.

What is Heaven? [Better as Heavens]

So, the Heavens are actually the milky Air hanging over this physical earth and are made into Spheres, beginning with the first Heaven (Gen. 1:1), then the second heaven (Gen.1:8), and all other spheres that came about later, including Satan's Enclave.

It is made into several hundred spheres. Each sphere represents a certain activity in the Heavens—a communication center, a manufacturing center, a refreshing/resting center, etc.

Since the Heavens are in a downward arrangement, these spheres are arranged from the first Heaven to a part of the entire milky world called the Lithosphere. [This is the Spiritual Lithosphere that gives sustenance to the kind of Lithosphere science talks about.] This type of heaven borders the ground with the Dew that wets our soil and the heavy winds that blow out things.

These are three spheres, examples of the many that make up the Milky Air (the World) of the Spirits.

It is in this part of the Milky Air that Satan lives, and this is the reason why He is considered the closest force hanging over this earth's crust. So, this allows Him to intercept all communications going to and coming from God.

So, God gave me a story of what He called the "Communication Superhighway," which explains how Satan intercepts the thoughts of man's heart and by that he, Satan, also responds to such thoughts to satisfy those who are burdened with them and by this means people who think about doing evils for wealth are given the ideas/tricks by Satan. Still, when this happens, people believe that God has blessed them. Oh no, God says to me He doesn't give anybody the thoughts of how to kill to get rich or how to prostitute to get rich and how to do all the things that do not fall in His good standards. They are all from Satan's Kingdom, which sits very close to the earth, where he ceases the thoughts from the hearts of people who desire the world he controls. The word "World" here is used in the context of 'things of the world.'

This Milky Air in which Satan lives is the Spiritual Lithosphere (soft part) of what science usually calls the earth's crust or solid part of the earth.

The powers of the earth's crust reside in the Lithosphere. The earth receives these forces in the form of rain, the sun, the moon, and darkness, each with its own subsidiary.

So, all that is referred to as the Garden, Satan, and these

men called Adam & Eve were and are still in the Spiritual World.

The spiritual man (Adam and Eve) is used as the medium to connect with the physical man, the duplicate. Both the male and female mediums are generally our human ancestry. Every angel knows how to get to them and how to use them.

Thankfully, human science has given us the TV and its remote. The remote communicates with the TV. Also, human science has given us an integrated system so that two or more devices can communicate.

The TV and its remote scenario explain how the Spiritual man is used as the remote for the Spirits [God and His angels, both good and bad] to communicate with the physical man on earth. Similarly, they use integrated technology [God and angels, both good and bad] to make both male and female humans communicate.

Furthermore, there are two kinds of men in the Heavens. First, in the Heaven above, God keeps for Himself the original copies of everything He created, and in the heaven below (the Garden), He has photocopies of everything He made in the Spirit World. This can be explained by current human technology, whereby creations can be duplicated with one original and one or more duplicates somewhere.

Look, what I'm describing here is the same as when science creates an object and then creates what to use to manipulate it so that the object may be far away from the owner, but he/she would have the ability to control it from a distance. So that which controls the object is called a "remote," but with God, it is the original, while the object being controlled is the duplicate/second part.

So, the Spiritual man [shadow Man] God threw out with Lucifer were the second souls [male and female called Adam and Eve] who were growing yet [undergoing training] in the Garden [a nursery or training ground].

This is not different from what God did by keeping the Souls of the Angels with Himself for His own purpose, including Satan, to use so that He is able to do anything to any of them at any time He wants to. And because He has every original part of everything keeping to Himself that He had made, He possesses the ultimate power to destroy all He had made at His will.

Can you imagine what man does with human science? Everything mankind creates with his hands, the same he has the ability [tools and knowledge] to destroy quickly. Also, everything man makes has the designs, originals, and copies of it. How couldn't God do all man does? It would be foolish for anyone to think God is incapable of knowing more than mankind does.

Evil in the Garden, Gen. Chapter 3

Right after the creation of the woman, evil entered the heart of Lucifer (often called "Satan"). The new word 'Evil' means "Evolvement of ails".

The "Evil" that occurred in the Garden of Eden is Lucifer's new attitude. Lucifer turned away from carrying out God's instructions and began to act on his own. [In science, this is called going out of control by equipment/robot.]

So, Lucifer went to man (Adam and Eve), first met Eve, and touched her with instructions not due to them then. [This again is interpreted in the word of science as missing the timing.]

This means there was a plan of God to teach man certain things to do, but God set a time to do so. This appeared in the words of Lucifer to the man, and He said, "You shall not surely die, Gen. 3:4; for God does know that in the day you eat from it, then your eyes shall be opened, and you shall be like gods, knowing good and evil, Gen. 3:5.

This act of Lucifer teaching man knowledge before the right time was by itself an interruption to God's plan for mankind. It was also an act of Lucifer taking God's Power for himself, which also means He did it His way but not the way of God. It was called a Rebellion (turn away from the right). So, God changed His name from Lucifer to Satan to mean "turned away from the right path or turned against the laws [the laws of Heavens governing everything.] And He took another name called "Devil," which means – Do evil [Do ails.]

This devilish attitude really angered God. So, God did not only get upset with Satan but also with man because God had already given man His own Will, the Power needed to resist evil. [Will-Power here can be simplified in science as 'Sensor.' A sensor on equipment is the sensing, detecting, or feeling part of that equipment. That part is responsible for preparing the equipment for action, whether to reject or accept, depending on how the sensor is programmed.] Therefore, God rejected the two (Satan and Man) from His presence. The man then had to pick up the long journey of suffering under Satan's control outside God's control area.

From this point in the Bible, God's spoken words embodied two things: His real Will and the will of the new leader of the world today. This means that from the time Man fell, God's speech has not been 100% clean of what man's practice has been on earth because He endorsed the idea of Satan's leadership due to man's own stubborn behavior.

God's endorsement is evident from the fact that He permitted Man to go out of the Garden to face the temptations of. Satan. It is further demonstrated in the Book of Job, wherein it occurred that Jehovah God conversed with Satan as to whether He had seen Job doing well in the world.

Job's case, however, is a physical & Spiritual example involving God's test of man's faith to persevere in resisting Satan while it also tells physical men that every man needs to keep hoping on God, whether or not Satan will force the man's life out of him.

Yes, Job's test is also a proof by God to this world that among millions/billions of people is one man that is fighting it hard with Satan. This man is worth trusted by Jehovah God because he is some 90% perfect as regards his thinking and attitude towards God, the rest is counted against his mortal flesh that expresses fears, pains, thirst & hunger. [Remember the fear for pains on the cross of Calvary that Christ expressed before his arrest, saying, "Oh Father, let this cup pass over me, but let your will be done!

[-Matt.26:38 & 39; Lk. 22:42 & Mk. 14:34 & 36. This cry for pain represents his human nature with mortal flesh.]

When we say God's perfect speech has become mixed up, we mean He sometimes grants people their will even if He was not ready to do so, like in Gen.3:21: "Unto Adam also and to his wife did the Lord God make coats of skins, and clothed them." Gen.3:22: "And the Lord God said, behold, the man is become as one of us, to know good and evil: and now, he must not be allowed to put forth his hand, and take also of the Tree of Life, and eat, and live forever."

These scriptures above present two situations that we need to look at critically. (1) God's action in Gen.3:21 came after Satan had first taught man the knowledge that God was not ready to give. Even though He clothed man in Gen. 3:21, (2), He gave a strong warning to the Angels not to allow a man to take also the "Tree of Life" in Gen. 3:22, and He said to the Angels, if you do so, you will make the man live forever like us.

What is critical to grasp here is that God agreed to clothe man in 3:21 because Satan had already done it. This is interpreted by 3:22 as God's unwilling gift. He did not want it to happen, but it happened, and so He accepted it as Satan's will that prevailed.

This further means when God speaks, but man cannot obey, then God often leaves man to his will to follow the ways of Satan. This explains why we continue to live even while we still sin.

God saw Satan's world ahead.

God is all-knowing, so He saw the kind of world that was coming after His perfect kind.

Immediately after God had made woman, He spoke about the practice of marriage to be on earth, and He said, "Therefore," –meaning "**because I made woman**" a man shall leave his mother and father to cleave unto his wife-Gen.2:24.

The above scripture predicted that the earth would take women into possession by men in the name of marriage (maturity age), which is different from how life exists in the Heavens. Jesus exposed this in Matt.22:30, saying, "For in the resurrection they neither marry; nor are given in marriage, but are as the angels of God in heaven." This Matt. 22:30 was given to me as an example of how the practices of this earth are not conformed to the practices of Heaven. The Spirit did not provide the verse, but the Spirit told me Jesus talked about marriage not being in Heaven and said to me whatever is not in Heaven that is on earth is not the perfect Will of God, but rather the will of His rebellious children.

And then the Spirit said, so Jesus told us [mankind] to pray the Lord's Prayer saying, "... let thy Kingdom come, and let your Will be done on earth as it is in Heaven."

> *Now, if Jesus asked for the Will of God to come down to be done as it is done in Heavens, and the lecture story in Mtt. 22:30 tells the heavenly living, then it is clear that what is happening on earth is not God's valid will.*
>
> *It was one of the reasons why Jesus kept telling his people about the ails of traditions. That is, the present system of things is not pleasant to God, but Jesus tried to be very tactful on them because he knew that the proper time had not come yet to change them.*
>
> *So, he always told them he came to fulfill them [but the conflict had been he kept criticizing the very things he said he did not come to change.*
>
> *This is the truth that the true Will of God is one system of marriage, one system of religion, one system of language, one system of knowledge of invention..., [all yet to come in the Kingdom come].*

Let me say this before people start to judge:
Marriages, which are divided according to different languages and traditions are binding until this system passes away.
The reason is that man is still bound to live under cultures and traditions that were introduced to him by Satan and his men of the air even before God came to earth.

[Full knowledge of how the gods of our lands (Satan and his men) introduced cultures & traditions to all people have been explained in my first book, "The Book of Interpretation First."]

What does the Garden stand for?

The Garden of Eden has three basic names, each given according to its purpose at a particular point in time.

1). It is called '**Lower heaven**' because it is a Spiritual World in which God originally stationed His angels as His assistants in running the activities of the earth. (2). It is called the 'Garden' because it depicts the earth's vegetation, creatures, and resources as God wanted it. (3). It is called a **'factory'** because God used it at the beginning of creation to teach the angels how to create, too. [In this way, the angels learned how to make the frame [body] of man but not his life. They also learned how to make all other living things.

Because they knew how to create like God, they became small gods. He visited this lower part of His Throne to see what work was done at all times.

Because the Heavens are the dwelling places for the Spirits, as they are living creatures, the lower heaven automatically becomes God's second estate, where the angels predominantly reside. It is two times larger than the Upper Heaven, God's Throne.

The word 'Garden' is just another name for a special place where God nursed the first man and trained the angels. He visited the place all the time to interact with the forces of the earth. It is God's own industrial City where manufacturing takes place. Communication has a base there, too.

It is also more like a storehouse of God where a photocopy of everything that is made is kept, and in this place, duplication is made possible to keep making new things and people.

Now, I want you to understand natural
Science so that you can rightly be on the
path to understanding this allegory (use of
symbols) for the names 'Adam & Eve.'
They are spiritual people still living in the
Spiritual World. They are our ancestral
roots.

They have been shown as falling from the right
path. They were thrown out of God's
gracious place, where they ate. freely.
Generations have sprung up from them,
and sins have begun to multiply.

Sufferings and killings have their roots with
them because of their attitude towards
God.

Spiritual generations represent how a single man shall bring to earth a whole nation; that is, one man can bear two, and the two can be responsible for four or more till they do not know themselves anymore as being of one man's lineage.

They shall also travel all over the earth and become different masters of arts & crafts. Still, among them shall be poor and rich as the nature of good and evil shall impact them individually.

Analogy of Conflict in the Garden

The Garden conflict is the beginning of the Spiritual wars that went on between the good ones of God and the bad ones of God. Both the angels and the man remain the forces of God, and the way everything happens is what the earth continues to receive.

God used my Country, Liberia, to demonstrate heavenly divisions.

The people in Liberia can easily understand this analogy.

They once enjoyed peace, but suddenly they broke out into civil war.

The war came about when a small group decided to rule, too. So they went out of the capital city (Monrovia) and founded another country they called "Greater Liberia," with a capital city they also Called "Gbarnga."

The Monrovia-based Liberians remained under another leadership. The split, therefore, placed the two groups of Liberians under two Presidents: rebel leader Charles Gangay Taylor for the Greater Liberia and Interim leader, Amos Sawyer, for the Monrovia government.

However, the rebel group of Liberians went out of the national government with their expertise. So, they founded a government that had engineers who built weaponry & communications systems, doctors who ran hospitals, teachers who taught young people, as well as economists who set up tax systems, etc.

They became a world of their own, and they fought the internationally accepted leadership.

Similarly, in the beginning, there was one peaceful group of God's children called the angels. They broke apart when one member (Lucifer) chose to do things by himself.

He recruited other angels and led a rebellion against God's Will.

They went out of the Garden (God's main city for the angels) and established their enclave called "Aquebus" with Capital City "Babel" [this is the Babel reported in the Bible (Gen. 11:1-9.) It is not a physical story. If it were physical, that means the construction of skyscrapers we see today would have started in ancient times since the early men were capable of building a house that rose above the skies.

The building may have collapsed, but the knowledge couldn't have been lost.

The Babel story is also a report of the Spiritual Science of technology. There is more on this ahead.

They went out of Heaven with every knowledge they. acquired from God during their training time in the Garden. So, they have been exhibiting their talents from the Spirit Realm [Babel event] to the human world [inspiring technology] since that time.

Christ has been loyal to God and continues to enjoy the good support of the Great God. He has been leading troops against Satan's Kingdom refers to this age. The result is trouble and confusion for mankind in the world.

In my other book title, The Book of Interpretation First, Satan and his collaborators called "The gods of Our Lands" have been fully discussed as a government that has been responsible for so many things [what modern people would call good things in science] and so many bad things in the same science of technology. That's why we have the science of weapons of mass destruction and drugs inhibiting death, while the same science gives us comfort with the air-cooling system, cars for mobility, etc.

Introduction to Early Man

Genesis Chapter 9

The Flood is reported in Chapter 8, but it gave birth to Chapter 9. So, let's See what it means before we proceed.

The Flood is just a short period that showed a transition between Spirituality and Physicality. It can equally be viewed like 'Birth' between Gestation (fetus development in the womb) and 'Existence' (growing up outside the womb).

This is the greatest mystery of man's evolvement into this world that many men of science have been looking for.

The Bible has the answer, but it has never been interpreted correctly since it occurred.

WHY? Because the writer of Genesis did not teach the Book. He died earlier than he could have lived to teach his people sufficiently.

Instead, most of the pieces of his scripts were picked up from different places as the Israelites wandered due to situations. Some of them tried to provide self-interpretations to what he received from the Great God.

The result has been self-imaginations that theologians hold on to. They are still finding answers to this book, but they behave like they know it best. Now, this is an opportunity for all peoples of both science and theology.

How the process occurred is explained in the end of this section.

So, through the Flood, the Spiritual world of Man ended, and the physical man came to be. The scripture, "From dust cometh man," was fulfilled when the spirits of mechanics [mech-anics] first played their creation role. They covered the spiritual beings (The souls of the male and the female) with mud after the dried ground became soaked with rainwater during the Flood period. As a result, man's physical body is composed of two main parts:

the spiritual man (**a man's living soul**) and the physical man [man's body (flesh & bones).]

Now, see that the soul is spiritual and thus belongs to the Spirit. Physical man cannot see nor touch it. It can be tampered with by any spiritual being or force. It holds up the flesh and bone to exist (that is, it is the body component that contains 'Life'). It can be taken to heaven for duplication, and God shall receive it for judgment because it doesn't die even after the flesh goes off it, which is why it lives in the Spirit Realm; Rev. 6:9-11, Eccl. 12:7.

As for the flesh and bone, they belong to physicality and are thus touchable & seeable by man. They are perishable and bound to decay. They contain 'pains, fear, thirst, hunger, joy, etc..' They are subordinate to the spirit.

The Early Man (Ape-Like Man)

The Bible reports that Noah and his family were the first to live on this earth after the Flood had subsided. This means Noah and his family shared two separate histories and identities with two different worlds.

First, Noah is a descendent of Adam and Eve, and we've learned that Adam & Eve lived in the Garden of Eden, which Ezekiel 28:13-17 tells us is not on this earth but is above the earth, which also means that it is a Spiritual world in which Satan, then Lucifer, interacted with them. And when they disobeyed God, they were thrown out of the Garden to the earth along with Satan. Then we learned that Satan is a Spirit that lives in the Spirit world, which tells us that the earth that Satan and man (Adam & Eve) were thrown to is not physical earth as have been understood earlier through human perception.

If we accept this analysis, then we're on the right path to

understanding that all the human characters, from Adam & Eve to Noah entering the Ark, are spiritual characters that didn't live as physically as we do today. [Later, we shall prove what made Noah a spiritual character.]

So, while first Noah and his family lived as spirits in Satan's Enclave after God had abandoned them, they were nurtured into the ways of Satan. They were earlier taught what skills they were born with at a later time, which were their cultures and traditions. That means that when God created mankind, Adam & Eve, He put in them powers that constitute their ability to choose right from wrong, and when they lived with Satan, they also obtained other powers that constitute their ability to rebel or follow the lifestyle of Satan who adopted them. The result for mankind is that he carries within him two opposing powers: the power to say okay to what is suitable for God and the power to say okay to what Satan likes.

Then, while the generations of Adam & Eve were yet in the Spirit realm, the time came for God to fulfill His creational decision at the maturity age of the man He had made. This means it was time for the Spiritual man to become physical (hard in form) to fulfill his actual duties of cultivating the physical earth to help maintain the Heavens. So, God had to end that world in which Satan led mankind to greater heights of disobedience. This is when God chose one man (Noah) out of that generation of those who were alive, and He gave instructions to the man to build a large boat that would float on top of the water that was about to fill the earth [all this taking place in the Spirit realm as the physical man had not been formed yet.]

Therefore, when the time came for God to create physical man, the Spirit of God moved (sprinkled the seeds of all human colors) on the face of the earth to form the physical man out of the soil He had made.

So, while the ground remained soaked with water, the spirits of mech-anics came down and moved all over the earth (sprinkled the seeds of three human colors). After that, humankind began to form from the soil, like a plant sprouts from the ground. In this way, every human type (white, semi-white, and black in their local varieties) residing in the Spirit realm was formed from the earth in different parts of the world. They germinated out of the ground one by one, just like plant seeds shoot out of the soil one by one after man has sown the seeds into the soil.

First Description of Human Evolvement

Because they sprouted from the soil like plants do every day, they couldn't walk upright right away; instead, they crawled on their bellies in the mud, and after a long period, they stood up to walk out of the mud but curved with hunched backs, then after another long period they walked upright. [Does this resemble the same stages every newborn human being goes through? YES, still, in our case, a baby must lie flat on the ground, crawl on its legs with hunchback (some on their bellies), and finally, learn how to walk straight up.]

Each of these stages counts for a generation of mankind. That means early man changed severally in body forms, structure, and stature over several thousand years. The early man we're talking about now is the one the Bible puts in the parable as Noah.

The meanings of Noah's activities

Noah's entering the Ark is the start of a Spiritual process that culminated in the forming of the physical being, and God instructing Noah to go into the Ark is like a man having sex to start a process of duplicating his/her body. Noah's stay in the Ark is like the gestation period of an embryo. Noah's coming out of the Ark is like the delivery process of a fetus. Noah's lack of ability to build objects from the start of the world system is like a newborn that cannot do things for itself. Noah's building of an altar for making sacrifices to the Lord (God) when he (Noah) was yet a young human baby who lacked knowledge was his heart's desire (his imagination) to build an altar to make sacrifices unto God for Thanksgiving.

This act of young Noah wanting to construct is like every young baby (from crawling to walking stage without clear speech) we see around the world that behaves like wanting to do things like mature people do. But this is what God wrote to tell how mature humans would offer sacrifices to God and the spirits.

The Stages of Early Man

The third thing that made me believe and that enhanced my strength so much is the Evolution of man.

I was told that man evolved from the mud right after the Flood. When he first emerged, he was like a young baby who could not walk but had to crawl on its belly or knees.

Does this remind you of something about babies? Yes, when a baby begins to walk, it does not walk straight up, and so did Early Man, who evolved.

The Spirit said he was like a Chimpanzee that crawled on its knees, but he was taller than the real Chimpanzee we know today.

I was told that just as a baby goes through several stages of growth, so did Early man. Then I was told to search world history for Early man, whose story is rightly told by science, unlike what the Bible users think was an instant occurrence and how man became what he is today.

So, in 2012, I was blessed to come across the report "On the Natural History of the Man-Like Apes (1863)."

Many of them are discussed in that publication, but the ones in Fig. 6 are named by the writer, "Linnaeus," from left to right, as 1. Troglodyta Bontii; 2. Lucifer Aldrovandi; 3. Satyrus Tulpii and 4. Pygmaeus Edwardi.

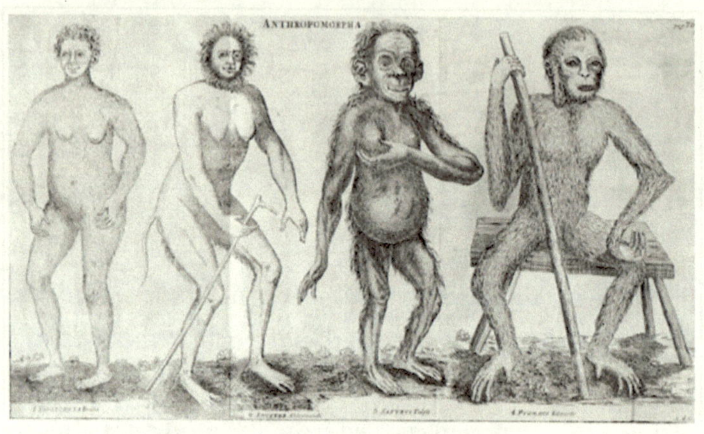

Fig. 6.–The Anthropomorpha of Linnæus

This group of early men shows the metamorphic transition that we referred to in this book as 'generations' from the Chimpanzee-like human to modern man, from furry to hairy and bent to upright.

Oh yes, I love this depiction of Natural History.

How Did Mankind Learn Things For The First Time?

So, when this early man [The Spirit said the Bible called him "Noah with a family"] first came out, he had no scientific knowledge until a particular generation [after him and his family] began to receive information from the forces of the Spirit world as to what to do and how to do it [even though they had powers in them already but the powers being seeds planted in them needed to be watered or nurtured in the physical world.] This means he earlier communicated like a young babe that communicates with the spirit until at a certain age [the age is the stage at which each babe begins to pronounce words to start communication with physical men.]

This also means that during this babyish stage, the very first humankind did not know how to make things. This is why Noah's act of building an altar for making sacrifices to the Lord (God) when he (Noah) was a young human baby represents his heart's desire. It was his imagination, just like a young baby nowadays would imagine (desire) doing something for its mother. Everything represents his heart's desire to build an altar to make sacrifices unto God for Thanksgiving.

Later, another early generation started receiving instructions from unseen forces that led them through the ways of doing things. This is why we see scientists continuing to invent things. An early scientist may hear voices, see things in space that no one else could see, or even dream dreams to do certain things. That process of making things into physical forms is now referred to as human science and has grown into many phases from generation to generation.

The Flood is a Parable, so what does it Mean?

Let's summarize this Noah issue before we proceed.

According to the Bible, he lived in the old world and started this new world that we live in today. In the old world, he built a boat that looked like what we can now call a ship. While constructing the boat, he used an axe [dagger], cutlass [machete], cutting saw, nail, or glue to do his work. Later, he came out of the boat to start the world we live in today. He used an axe [dagger] to break wood to offer a sacrifice to God after he came out of the boat.

Looking at all his achievements above means he knew how to construct boats and make working tools. However, this first human on earth, who knew how to do these things before starting the New World, didn't build the first canoe or boat in human history. The history of inventions didn't begin with the first humans [the ones science called early men] after the so-called Flood. Rather, those inventions came thousands of years after the first humans. So, Noah can't be a physical man who started our world system.

This means that the Flood is a parable [Allegory of the transition between two different worlds] of changing from first human existence to second existence, commonly put as the end of a world in which the Soul was prepared to come to live on physical earth. In contrast, the building of an "Ark" in the first world's last days became a symbol of a time in the life of the second world's last days' generation [physical man's last day's generation] that will have science reaching its highest peak of building a large ship called "Aircraft carrier."

The Aircraft carrier would be a huge ship that will have the capacity to carry any size of an animal, a large number of foodstuffs, many people, every type of vehicle regardless of size, and [particularly] a flying machine that may be sent out into the land to take pictures and record information to bring back to the ship. The flying machines would be used to go into the lands to collect food to bring on board to feed the crew.

Theologians are now ready to argue it out, but this is what the Spirit said: If the first world was as physical as ours today, and then the Ark was indeed a physical object built by a physical man, then it means that second Noah [Noah after the Flood] must be put on record as the father of scientific inventions, or better still he must have taken aboard all of the tools he used to build the Ark in the first world that he may have started with the second world [the world in which you and I live now]. He must have also known from the very beginning of our world system how to build shelters & ships, how to make nails, how to make machetes, and how to break wood into lumbers/planks from the start of our generation since, indeed, he had already received the science of building objects from God in the first world.

But given the fact that everything man knows today started at nothing but later became known and grew into stages over the periods that man has been in existence, it is evident that the second Noah [a man who (supposedly) started the first generation of people that we came from], didn't invent nails, machetes, or even begin the breaking of woods into lumbers/flat boards, neither did he build and live in a cabin. Instead, history tells us that the first humans lived in caves and hollows of woods.

In fact, if Noah [the first human being on earth] had known how to build such a gigantic boat as attributed to physical existence, don't you think the Stone Age generation should have been the ones to have advanced in science such that they must have had the level of technology we have by the year 2018 while by this time 2018 we must be more advanced in technology [more than talking about having 5G technology] now?

Therefore, the revelation I received during my time in the School of the Spirits told me that the Ark of Noah is simply an allegory (a symbol) representing modern Science. This means that the building of Noah's Ark marked the end of the old world's Science of building sophisticated objects. That is, the World of the Spiritual Human (from Adam to Noah) ended with the sophistication of the Science taught by Lucifer.

Interpretations of the Ark symbols

Please take a keen look at the two pictures below before proceeding. They are two of the several works that show carpentry skills that people have been displaying to the world. But what is essential for discussion concerning the matter at hand is that there are varying presentations (photos) that the various reporters have been showing, which means that there is no definite description of the Ark, which means the Ark is yet a mysterious object that has hidden facts surrounding it. And that's why my book is here to reveal those mysteries.

A

B

Royalty-free stock photo ID: 707147620

https://pixabay.com/photos/netherlands-dordrecht-ark-clouds-929117/ *Several other photos are available online, such as this link: Noah's Ark 1865 | Great Big Canvas*

So, I'm very eager to know how these photos came about, whether the people built them as new models for the Ark of Noah or, better still, which of them is precisely how the Ark looked like.

So, I keep pondering which picture portrays the actual look of the Ark of Noah.

Still, another more interesting one is not royalty-free, so I cannot include it in my book. That one, they said, was found on Mount Ararat in 2002 by a group of researchers who made an archaeological report on the discovery of Noah's Ark.

My interest is drawn to what they said about the age of Noah's Ark. They said that by the year 2002, the Ark was about 4,300 years old. That's how old the object that they said to have found is, and it is the same that they could interpret exactly as what they sketched out and built to show the world.

So, apart from what the spirit told me about the Ark and

its components, I did a Google search on one of the materials that made up this beautiful ark from the work of the archaeologists. I researched about nails.

My research found that Nail was about 2,000 years old by 2002, and the Ark, they said, was about 4,300 years old by the same year.

So, the question I pose is: How possible was that nail used to build the Ark? If you do the mathematical calculation, you'll come to know that there is a difference of 2,300 years between the age of the Ark and that of the nail.

All the woods used in every picture were sawed into lumber/planks and nailed with hammers. The other question about the saw and hammer is: When were they first invented, and by whom, Noah or somebody later?

Well, it's evident that people have been guessing about the actual look of the Ark; that's why there are different models. That is because there is a mystery surrounding the Ark story, which must be unveiled before all the guessing stuff ends.

However, a few things must remain constant about the Ark description Moses made in Genesis. For example, Moses said the Ark was built in three stories on the order of God [Genesis 6:16 reads (NIV) "Make a roof for it, leaving below the roof an opening one cubit high all around. Put a door in the side of the ark and make lower, middle, and upper decks."]

I suppose this is the pattern that every emulator follows to construct a model that is displayed to the human public for the Ark.

With this wide margin of about a 2,300-year difference, I

hardly find it possible to accept that the picture actually represents the Ark of the Bible but to make believe that what was dug up must have been the fossils of one of the old-time boats.

Now, God has revealed the hidden secrets of the Ark to me. He said it is not a physical object, nor was it built by a physical man or by the first human being on earth when our world system started. Instead, it symbolizes many things in our physical world today, including impregnation, gestation, birth, babyhood, and the science of technology.

Therefore, God commanded me to tell the story of how man started as a spirit man who first lived in the Spirit world where he saw God and interacted with Him, where everything was freely disposed to him, where he was given laws by God [his Father] to obey, where he was deceived and swayed by God's subordinating force and where he was banished before becoming physical.

As a spirit man, he lived longer years than any physical man. And as a spirit man, he bore children, and he had generations of children. While living in the spirit world, he acquired knowledge and became sophisticated before becoming a physical man. Because he transitioned between two different worlds, he had to start everything all over again like his ancestor father [Adam] did.

How the Bible became exact on everything

The Bible told us stories of yesterday [Early centuries] about what would happen in the future [thousands of years after] because it was delivered unto mankind as a report of several events about two different worlds; the first world [Man's spiritual existence] and the second world [Man's physical existence]. So, what we have as biblical predictions became the retelling of events that occurred in the past that would occur for the second time because the same forces would continue to act on the physical man.

So, the Spirit of God told me that since the building of a large boat (Ark) represents how advanced the Spiritual man was in his end time, physical man is also building large vessels [boats/ships] as a show of their advanced knowledge in human science at the end time of their existence.

Now, here are the meanings of things in the Ark's story: The animals and men entering into the Noah Ark and later surviving the Noah Flood are now the same as man putting all kinds of animals and creatures in a boat or ship today. The birds of Noah's Ark that flew into the land and brought back food now represent the airplanes that fly from those ships to the lands and bring food to the crew. The birds of Noah's Ark also went into the land to spy if there was a chance for the crew (Noah and his family) to get off the ship to continue their lives on earth, which currently represents the airplanes that fly into the lands to spy for settlement, especially during flood time or war time. Can you see the small flying object called a drone today that can be sent from a ship in the deep sea to go into the land to take pictures or bring things to the ship in our end times?

Thus, Noah and a few people surviving the first World will be the same at the end of our time. A few persons shall remain alive at the end of the world (the Bible called it the 'Rapture Time'), and they will become new people in the new world that Christ will rule.

Early Man's Living Conditions

In the Holy Book of Genesis chapter 9, Noah's generation is reported to have known drinks and worn clothes at the beginning of our system, but it was God's wise saying called 'Allegory' (**a work in which the characters and events are to be understood as representing other things and symbolically expressing a deeper, often spiritual... senses.**)

It means that the first generation of early people [Noah kind of people] didn't actually know human Science that deals with invention/creation, so they couldn't have had drinks [They didn't know how to manufacture drinks or anything]. Instead, they simply ate certain fruits that contained alcohol content that hypnotized them, and they wore garments made of leaves.

This symbolic expression about what life they lived brings the beginning of physicality (Second Noah – a physical man) into similarity with the beginning of Spirituality

(Adam – a spiritual man) or, to say, brings the beginning of the first world into similarity with the beginning of the second world.

Let me simplify it more: The true fact is that in the beginnings of all things, man knew nothing. Neither Adam & Eve nor second Noah & his generation knew anything about science (the word of inventions.) Instead, they simply started to walk nude/naked and owned nothing until the spirit of God came and spoke out about what they needed to do, how to do it, and what not to do.

So, the Biblical saying that Adam & Eve made themselves aprons with fig leaves (Gen.3:7) now manifested physically as Noah & his generation wearing clothes (Gen.9:23), which were the real leaves they wore while their leafing clothes also represented real clothes to be manufactured from plants in the days of advanced human development since they emerged from the stage of incubation to doing their own things.

Another saying is that Adam & Eve ate freely from the Garden (Gen.2:16), also manifested as Noah & his generation (Ancient men) who ate wild fruits and animal flesh from the jungles in which they roamed, for they had no method of sowing seeds nor cooking food in the beginning.

If anyone wants to argue that Adam & Eve and second Noah & His generation truly lived like us by wearing clothes and drinking wines, as well as building boats with planks and nails/glues-using blade saws and hammers, cutlasses [machetes] and axes [daggers]; then let him prove by science when the invention of wine and clothes... started for it is possible that archaeologists get the fossils of irons that made up components of their industrial machines since indeed they must have had such industries similar to ours today.

Once again, for emphasis; we continue to say that the first world was a spiritual preparation of things to happen in the physical world and thus ended with first Noah & the Flood, while the physical world in which we are today started with the second Noah (**a metamorphosed man**) and is now heading to its end with every good and evil that took place in the first world except that there wouldn't be a Flood again, but there would be an intense heat, 'Fire', of mass destruction by fire of weaponry. [The fire of weaponry that shall reduce human population to the lowest ever shall be like the Flood that reduced Spiritual humans to their lowest population, thus making just a few (Noah and his family) to reach the time of metamorphosis (changing form), which is how a few physical men and women shall reach the time of re-metamorphosing from physical to Spiritual to face judgment, separation, punishment & freedom, then restoration]. This will happen as a fetus goes through stages of development in a half-spiritual world [called living in the womb and the early living as a baby outside the womb]. That is exactly how man passed through several stages of development to become what he is today.

Science and Religion Meet

Genesis Chapter 10

As you start this topic, I must admit that this is one of the most challenging topics I have been trying to make clear to everyone. So, please bear with me and read everything until you reach the end. You may understand by taking them in whole, not in pieces.

In this chapter, the Bible reports that mankind began to populate the earth. God uses Noah and his sons to show how the human population process started, but let's analyze this to see if there isn't something to be corrected here since I was told that it is another parable of God showing us how one man would have many children, who would grow into a large population that would comprise both bad and good and travel far away to meet other people.

I will discuss this in depth when I discuss the issue of blackness. However, this generation didn't have the capacity [knowledge] to build houses or boats [unlike what the Bible described about them] since they were the first humans to start our world system, which is why they fit in the human species human science described as early men, who roamed the earth without clothes, fire, houses [living in caves and hollows of woods], etc.

This is the humankind the Spirit of God revealed to me in 2006-2008, saying the best way to understand what God revealed to Moses is to visit the science of anthropology, dealing with archaeological investigations of early men. So, to do this, we must deviate entirely from the Bible [Spiritual reporting] to go straight into science to discuss early men and their stages of development.

The reason we must leave the Bible [Spiritual reports] is that the Bible says Noah and his children lived in an old world where he (Noah) built an object he called an Ark. That object resembles the boats or ships we have in the 21st century. So, the Spirit said [IF] Noah had been a physical human being who had built a boat, then he must have known how to build houses and do many other things before the so-called Flood. The Spirit continued to say that IF he (Noah) possessed such sophistication, then he and his family should have immediately started our world system with inventions of all the things that came into the world later. That means he was the man who invented water vessels (canoe, boat, or ship) even before any subsequent recorded time of each invention, contrary to archaeological or anthropological reports of each invention. Thus, the Spirit said scientists attempted to provide the correct answer, while theologians were guessing it because they couldn't understand what Moses wrote. This is where science and religion meet.

Therefore, the early generation, beginning with the second Noah, was curved in stature, enabling them to walk lower to enter any holes found under high mountains. Their bodies were covered with fur hair that protected them from the colds of the open air they slept in and the bushes they crawled through. Their faces were long and hollowed, making them look like today's Chimpanzees. They were huge and tall in stature, so they were earlier described as giant men in the Holy book of Genesis 6:4.

This hugeness and tallness helped them to lift heavy stones and kill animals as large as elephants.

Tower of Babel

Genesis Chapter 11

Also, the Bible reports that mankind was building a house to reach Heaven. Let's analyze this to see if it was true about this human generation or if it is another parable of God predicting what mankind will do with human science in the future.

Let's go back to chapter 10, where it says Noah's children have spread out already, building nations in their languages [Genesis 10:1-31 {32 says: "These are the families of the sons of Noah, after their generations, in their nations, and by these were the nations divided in the earth after the Flood"}].

The point to understand is that they [the Bible writers] said in chapter 10 that Noah's children have spread out and have founded nations already, and they spoke in different languages already [Verse 5: "By these were the isles of the Gentiles divided in their lands; every one after his tongue, after their families, in their nations"].

So, in what part of the Bible did they come back together

as one people to start building a tall house to go to Heaven in chapter 11, after spreading out into nations and speaking different languages in chapter 10?

This is why the Spirit said the early people of God were confused over the things Moses wrote and left unexplained. They used their imaginations to fit the pieces together, which resulted in errors in God's word. These are errors of interpretation, not God's errors of reporting Spirituality along with half-physicality and physicality.

This is to say that the entire process of the Spirituality and physicality of man, which was given to Moses, can be put in the categories of a [1]embryo [early development stage in the womb], a [2]fetus [growing into a complete human in the womb], [3]baby [a complete human brought out of the womb and now living on earth but unable to do things for itself], [4]growing up [growth processes of crawling, sitting, learning how to walk, and walking but still not capable of doing things grownups do. Thus, God put all these and many more in one big parable that mankind considers a book called the Book of Genesis.

The first group of early men

The first group of human species on earth was not only the second Noah and his family of the Bible, but their story told to the Jews was used by God to symbolize how mankind became physical. Still, the Jews didn't properly tell the story rather than saying every humankind came from Noah's children. EMPHASIS: Noah was just one of humankind, so God used him to tell how every human being came into the world. The story shows how his children consisted of three colors [similar to how black people have very black, dust-black, and bright colors], how they spread out into different parts of the world to do intermarriages with other humans, etc.

While the people of the Middle East [from whom the Hebrews or Jews went into exile in Egypt] were growing up, there were other human species in other parts of the world, which is why Noah's son's generations started meeting other humans and fighting wars with them.

All these different peoples of the earth at the time really ate fruits freely and ate the flesh of animals they strangulated with bare hands because they all lacked scientific method [the idea of creation] at the onset.

This early lifestyle of primitive people [consistent with every race] was captured by human science [it was whispered to physical humans by the spirits of science or creation]. It reported how mankind developed ideas bit by bit until now, while at the same time, religion reported this same story in parables such as the Ark story, the Noah story, the Abraham coming to God story, and as mature people who knew how to make things.

This first group roamed the surface of the earth without any civilization; no clothes, no fire, and no implements and tools.

The second group of early men

The second group of people of the early man possessed similar stature as did the first group. This group developed some intelligence. They learned how to hunt and dig caves with sharp stones they found in deep valleys of volcanic areas. These were men of the earth who heard the voices of the spirits teaching them what to do and not to do, bringing out the seed of knowledge planted in them in the Spirit Realm when Lucifer showed the "fruit" to the Spiritual man (Adam and Eve) and trained their generations before the Flood of transformation occurred.

The first two groups (first generation and second generation) covered a period of human development that was between Spirituality and Physicality. They behaved like a young baby does today when it sees things in the Spirit or puts on smiles or giggles with Spiritual forces, while in some moments, the same baby tends to smile or laugh with its mother, which are signs that it communicates with both Spiritual and Physical existences.

This means the first two generations of human existence on earth, which are exemplified [allegorized] by Noah & his three sons in the Jewish historical book of the Bible [herein described as the first group of humans] and Noah's grand-children [also described as second group of people on earth] roamed [as nomads] from place to place in the Mesopotamia area as did other human species [Races] in other parts of the world without having sophisticated human intelligence to do physical construction as opposed Jewish assertions about Abraham, whom they say built an altar to sacrifice his son.

Coming to the story of Abraham, I must admit that this is difficult for me to talk about, but the spirit continued to tell me that what Moses discussed in his writing was not exactly what the people ascribed to another Abraham in Ur. The Spirit said Moses' Abraham was not part of human civilization just as did Noah because they were part of the earliest humans who roamed the earth nude/naked and didn't no anything at all.

The question is: How many years between Noah and [Moses's] Abraham? If the years are calculated, then people must go to the second step to calculate the ages of all the classes of early humans on earth [Did anthropologists say Java man was the first or who?] until they can arrive at the first class of human who developed the first civilization of making tools to hunt and farm.

These calculations are necessary to determine whether the distance between the first human (Noah) and the Abraham Moses talked about makes Abraham fit into the class of people with knowledge of making axes and cutlasses since he broke wood to build an altar for offering a sacrifice.

The truth is: How Moses obtained the old stories [contained in the Book of Genesis] is just similar to what I'm doing today as I speak the words of the Spirit to clarify these allegories. These stories came to me when I was arrested strangely, and for two and half years, I listened to the voices of the spirits who told the stories. They called themselves lecturers or professors at the theocratic school [in the Spirit Realm] of the Spirit of the Lord Jesus. They didn't allow me to go to any theological school in our human world, just as they took Moses away from his people until he received the stories he wrote, which became the Book of Genesis later.

So, everything in the Book of Genesis was not any oral history that was passed on from one generation to another; rather, it was explained to Moses by the Spirit of God [like it happened to me in 2006-2008]. After Moses had listened to these stories while he was in a trance for 40 days and 40 nights, he wrote them as I am doing right now, but he didn't explain them as I will be doing from time to time before I leave this world.

The picture I'm painting here is for mankind to understand that the characters in Moses' Book of Genesis are not equivalent to everything we are. Rather, they were spirits and half-spirits.

The entire process of narrating where we came from, how we came here, and how we developed into different stages before we got to this point of modern people, is a complex situation combining Spirituality and physicality together. It is exactly what the spontaneous generative process goes through when we [humans] are formed in our mother's womb [concealed from the physical world yet], go through several stages of development in the womb, born into the physical world but seeing and talking with the spirits [babies are like that], growing up and talking with both the spirits and physical humans [when babies are learning how to speak the language of a tribe or people it was born in], and finally complete the three stages of early development [crawling, sitting, and walking] to participate in real life of doing things for oneself with or without someone's assistance.

It was not explained like this, so the early Christians discarded some of what Moses had written and left them behind. Those who gathered them couldn't understand them perfectly, so they wrote them in their own understandings, which is why they contradict human history, such as when inventions started and when something the Bible speaks about in Genesis actually happened, such as the building of boats or the making of axes (daggers).

Isn't it proper to say that the invention of the axe and the breaking of wood were not known for many centuries until certain groups of Abraham's generation gained the knowledge to do so, excelling in Egypt while in exile? Still, after so many other years of wandering by these early nomads, He [God] told these old stories to one of their own, Moses, while he was caught up in the Spirit. So, they would finally settle down in the place (now Israel) He had desired them to dwell in after He had granted them freedom out of slavery before allowing them to compile these stories together into books.

Because Abraham became one of the human beings who came at the end of the second group [a generation] of humans on earth [a group that started the period of human maturity], he was said to have been uncivilized yet incapable of melting bronze or iron, no agriculture, no pottery, and nothing to make him that man who built an altar to sacrifice a child to God. Rather, there was so much about his growing up that the people tried to piece together.

Also, God's use of Abraham's obedience of accepting to kill his son [listening to God's voice telling him to construct an altar] is an allegory explaining how the slaughtering of human beings on the altar for sacrifices to the gods of the earth would come into the world, but He (God) wouldn't participate in it by stopping Abraham from killing his son.

So, stopping Abraham in the story tells how God would put an end to human sacrifices [all human killings] in the days of the gospel. This was what Jesus fulfilled when he told Peter and others to put back their swords, saying to them, "No more of this." No more of this - was a reference to the wars Israel had been fighting before he (Christ) came to earth.

The third group of early men

The third group of people of the early man stood upright but a little bent over such that they looked like they had hunchbacks. They had less fur hair on their skins.

According to our gathering, this group discovered fire and blacksmithing. They also discovered pottery, and they baked clay pots. They also hammered stones into sharp blades that they hunted with and dug deeper into hills and mountains. They actually started what is now at its peak as technology {or technical knowledge of doing things.}

There were blacksmiths in Africa, Asia, Europe, and other parts of every continent using bellows to blow fire to heat metals. All these ideas didn't start in the Middle East alone, where the Bible put the first human being and it said he gave birth to every human race on earth.

The fourth group of early men
EXTRAS

The fourth group of people also stood upright and had less fur hair on their skins. They also carried with them all the skills of the third group of people. This group of early men is credited with an improved method of living. WHY? Because they did not live primarily in caves, but they started to build shelters with baked clay that looked like ovens, and in some lands, they built them with thatches.

Apparently, this is the group that my grandfather's generation came from when he said they lived in thatched houses.

These types of houses started as round with caw wood walls or round with mud walls. Earlier, they were built with no inside partitions, but later, the people began to cut partitions inside to make rooms.

When I was growing up, I lived in a thatched house, too. I participated in building my grandfather's last thatched house in the 70s. It was from this type of house that my grandfather built a zinc house in 1979/80.

Human science vs. religion

Comparing science and religion, science has more evidence of human development, while religion has little evidence because it speaks in parables. Thus, anthropologists give us a chronology of human development when they talk about the Homosapians and others or when they tell us about the different civilizations around the world, including the Bronze Age, Iron Age, Agricultural Revolution, Writing Age, Industrial Revolution, and other civilizations before technological periods came for us.

So, all these stages of human development and achievement can tell us that the first human didn't have anything until later when another group began to develop ideas, which mankind built on one after the other until now.

That's why the theory that Noah built a boat in the first world can be assigned to Spirituality without physical evidence since boat building didn't exist in his second life until later when other generations started it, which is why human history has hard truth, unlike biblical story about mankind with loopholes.

The Continental Drift

The clause "The Continental Drift" refers to dividing the world into its major Islands as they are today.

It is hard to explain nature, but it happened to be that the earth's mantle [earth's upper parts] was torn apart as the Stratos (hard parts) remained fluid but not solidified yet. The Stratos [hard parts of the under layers] were not affected. That's why some minerals are stretched beyond the borders of continents today. [The Spirit put the word " Stratos " on my tongue to mean the hard parts of the earth's crust].

But before then, the early men had begun to populate the earth. They started to spread out to the various parts of the earth by way of losing track of family members while in search of food or by fleeing wars and diseases at some point in time. As each member went away, some didn't return and thus continued to live somewhere different by themselves. Some that went in male and female pairs began to make new families, establishing new settlements from the largest group of the early people that flocked together. So, by way of the drift, small (very tiny) groups of people were occupying the islands (mainly known as Africa, Asia, Europe, and the Americas today).

The fifth group of early men [Modern Men]

As I became more stable (no longer wavering) about receiving information, it was revealed clearly to me on this day, Tuesday, March 19, 2019, that this generation really refers to us as 'Modern men.'

We're the ones who walk straight up today but have very few huge people in stature now. We have hairs on our bodies, but they are no longer fur-like. The shapes of our skulls don't fit into the chimpanzee group of animal classifications. We have grown more intelligent in masonry and have become too proud of our skills so much that we choose to go building houses in heaven [in Space] where God is because we're now fearing not to stay on this earth that is polluted with diseases and nearing human destruction.

Our group appeared in the Holy book of Gen. 11:1-9. The people Bible says they had built themselves a tower to reach Heaven, but to see how the Jews misunderstood the book of Genesis, let's start by analyzing the story of the

Tower of Babel, which is said to have been built and destroyed in Genesis chapter 11 when in fact there were nations and languages already in chapter 10.

> So, let's get something straight: Genesis chapter 10 comes before chapter 11.
>
> Now in chapter 10 Noah's three sons have already born children who built different cities and spoke different languages, including Ham's descendants who made up ancient Egypt, Canaan and Cush; all with their own languages.
>
> Particularly, chapter 10:4 gave account of Javan's sons – Elishah, Tarshish & Kittites "from whom the Maritime peoples spread out into their own territories by their clans within their ***nations***, each with its own ***language***."
>
> So, how then, in chapter 11 anyone could say that the people spoke one language until their building collapsed in that chapter 11 before different languages came on earth? Isn't that something was misunderstood from what Moses called the "Tower of Babel?"

Another misunderstanding in the book of Genesis is the origin of each race. The book doesn't give any account of which of Noah's three sons, the European man, Chinese man, Asian Indian man, American Indian man, Mexican man, Russian man, and other people, came from. Instead, theologians continued to strive well to put forth the theory that everybody came from the three sons of Noah.

Even though the Jews managed to insert a piece of story to talk about the origin of the black man, only whom they said came from the descendants of Noah's son, Ham.

However, the Spirit of God revealed that some Middle Easterners crossed the Red Sea to settle in the former Gojjam Kingdom of present-day Ethiopia. They are the ones whose generations still bear children of Middle Eastern identities at birth.

Now, the Spirit of the Almighty has seen this confusion among the people who interpreted Moses' work, so He clarified this matter to me.

He said the Babel Story is a description of the science of technology, which would come to the last days humans. They would exhibit the science of technology that was planted in Spiritual man while He was in Satan's city of Aqquebus with the capital city named "Babel/Babbel."

The Spirit of God said Moses wrote about this city without indicating that it was Spiritual, so his failure to indicate that he saw this city in the Spirit Realm, his successors thought that he was talking about a physical place [city] for the physical man who was formed after the Flood.

The Spirit said the Babel parable stands for the advanced human science [Technology] about constructing rockets [Space planes being constructed high into the skies] that the last days physical humans [Scientists] would use to go to the Moon or Mars [this is the heaven] where they'll want to live. This was the Heavens that the Spirit reported, which was written about in Genesis after the earth had been populated already [Genesis 10] by different peoples with different languages who were scattered all over the earth by the Spirit of mech-anics.

So, the interpretation given to this portion of the Bible (Gen. 11:1-9) is one of several human imaginative ways of understanding Spiritual things that seem like physical things all because Physicality is a direct replica of Spirituality.

Our group, therefore, remains the largest group of people inhabiting this earth. Because we stick together, with technological connectivity, we remain one people no matter where one person lives. So, we now have all the opportunity of sharing the ideas of going to space together [sharing technological ideas] to improving our individualities on earth [that technology language we speak all over the world makes us one people with one mindset].

But Satan controls the science of our present system, and he is a proud creature, so Jehovah shall rain His anger against our projects of building rockets to reach the heavens to live there. Therefore, the idea of living on the Moon or Mass or other outer spaces is the fulfillment of the physical Tower of Babel done by physical men and women of the earth today to relocate from the earth in search of a new living place.

The man who spoke to me in 2006-2008 said that the building crumbled to the ground as a result of one heavy storm that God sent across the city so that the people fell from the sky [this was His wisdom of telling our generation that not even living on the Moon is safe when the end comes].

He said His mystery beheld the people of Babel [Satan's capital city] like in the days of the apostles in the Upper room who spoke in many tongues without knowing how. This is how it shall be in the end when those who shall leave this earth to Space shall come crumbling down with insanity [many strange voices] that they shall call "languages" for the men of science. So, each person that understands one shall follow him or her, and they shall all be divided officially to let God's Will prevail still; saying, "Cursed is the woman and the man-Gen.3:16 & 17g – 19.

YES, Jehovah agreed to let man suffer to learn the hard way of doing things. And after that, He shall restore him (man) to His perfect way of life.

Why the Book of Genesis was so difficult to interpret?

Genesis 50 - Exodus

God had a plan for the people who originated from Abraham in the land of Ur [Ur, now in present-day Iraq] before they grew into a big group of the Hebrews people. And though they were taken into captivity in Egypt, God's plan remained ultimate, that no one would have thwarted it.

So, God had His way of implementing that plan step-by-step, such as when He [God] made the Egyptian King find favor in Joseph and let Joseph take his father's corps home to the land of Canaan.

And though the Hebrews remained slaves and maltreated in Egypt, the same God killed the sense of meanness in King Pharaoh's daughter, who took the young baby - Moses to her father's Palace when he came of age, where he learned all the things of the Egyptian people.

Was this not God's own trick of smuggling His own spy

into the same Palace that shall turn against the spy child? Was this not God's wisdom and man's stupidity? Yes, It was!

So, in God's mighty power, He suppressed the plan of the forces of evil that gathered in Egypt to thwart the manifestation of His [God's] power there, then changed the mind of the Egyptian King, Pharaoh, who decided to kill Moses who was among the male children of the Hebrews people. God preserved him.

Moses was nurtured under the culture of the Egyptians and thus became knowledgeable in all things of the palace by participating in every cultic initiation.

When he was initiated, he became fully accepted because they now believed that he could no longer go to his people to serve the God his people worshipped, but when the turning point came, the Spirit of God stirred Moses up, and he became violent against the attitude of the Egyptians. He had to commit murder, for God knew that it was the highest crime that could have turned the King and his people against the Hebrew child. They declared him an enemy, and Pharaoh demanded his arrest.

That was God's way of getting Moses out of Egypt to prepare him for the task he was born to bear.

Now, Moses left the palace at the Will of God. It was time to start the battle with Pharaoh to let the Hebrews go to the new land He (God) had chosen for them.

Another secret plan of God was never to let any family interfere in Moses' encounter, an encounter that was to take him many days to complete. Therefore, He sent Moses away from his wife and in-laws in his refuge land area of Midian.

So, Moses unknowingly [like a drunk] walked up Mount

Sinai. There, he saw God as Christ's 'Burning Bush'. Then the Spirit of God [Jehovah Yahweh] entered into Moses in the form of a smoke that choked him into a trance [a long sleep] for him to be cleansed of the filths [all the impurities] of Egypt.

Moses suffered the internal battle of the forces of good and bad in his body by vomiting, toileting, urinating, sweating, coughing, sneezing, and yawning out every evil power that was initially imputed into his body by the Egyptian gods & goddesses.

And while he was in that trance [a long sleep condition], he was taken up to Heaven, where he saw and was told everything that makes the Beginning of all beginnings - the Genesis.

So, the stories in Genesis were simply told by a Spirit (a Supernatural Being) but not on account of any oral or written history, and that's why it has loopholes/gaps in it that no physical man had ever understood until now that He [God] had raised another man to enlighten the world.

When Moses woke up, he was then given the laws that made the constitution of God and was thus given powers that gave him authority over the powers of the earth. These were the powers Moses displayed over Pharaoh's powers, used to feed the Jewish people in the wilderness and used to dry the Red Sea.

The signs [evidence] truly demonstrated God's superiority over the gods & goddesses of the earth – the same that He, God, placed in power in the beginning. The signs were also meant to cajole them [the Hebrews/Jews] into taking much interest in Him- GOD.

So, you see, how mysterious God is and has been and will always be?

He is and has always been in the business of working through Satan's wicked plans to accomplish His own plans because He is God, the Head of all powers.

However, all that God had done for the Hebrews or has done through the Hebrews, was to prepare the coming of His son [His Second Spirit or His duplicate] to live among mankind to physically meet and explain what Heavens is.

God didn't do all that to show the Hebrews that they were perfect or that they were better than others, but because they were made, the elects back in the Spirit Realm, even before the earth was formed. This is part of the story of 'the pre-earth human history.'

Real meanings of Spiritual things beginning at Adam

The first World people preach and talk about every day is the Root or Beginning of our physical world. Let me repeat this - it is a Spiritual world. Whether someone accepts it or not, it is the world of the Spirits.

The World of the Spirits started with their first human tools called Adam & Eve in the Bible and ended with the Noah [1st Noah who built the Ark] and His family. That is why the assertion that the first man on earth built such an object as the picture of the Ark we see every day is not fit to be true.

The biblical story that says Adam & Eve (first men) were naked and in later times were clothed is the symbol of how Noah (2nd Noah) and his family started naked and later clothed themselves with leaves as did the first physical men on earth.

The biblical story that Adam & Eve gave birth to a population of people that filled the earth is the symbol of Noah[2] and his wife, or every other man & woman to give birth to a population of people on this earth.

Disobedience to God's word in the Garden (the vegetative part of Heavens) is the symbol of disobedience in this physical earth covered with vegetation.

Killing of brother or fellow man (Abel and Caine) in the first world of the Spirit men is the same impacted unto us by the forces of evil that we're killing one another.

Harlotry and all forms of sexual malpractices experienced in the Spirit world (Sodom and Gomorrah) are the same that we see in our world today.

WHY? Because our world is simply a replica of the Spiritual. The way everything took place in that world after breaking away from God's commandments is the same sequence this physical world is going through as it approaches its end.

The same way God spoke to Noah to tell his generation [Noah's contemporary men] about what to do right when the end was near is how God has spoken to me (Paul-the storyteller) to tell my generation about the right things to do [go down to EXTRAS for the analogy on judgment and others].

The only difference that shall be is the kind of ending our world shall receive. Our world would end with fire. It is the fire of the weapons the nations are building slowly. The wars would not mark the complete end of this world; rather, they would scorch the earth to the ashes of the trees, and everything man has built and would reduce the human population to the lowest ever seen in this world. After almost everyone has died, then would come the rapture. The rapture is God's own process of ending every system on earth.

Comparison of human soul to plant soul/semend

The first world ended with Water because physical man needed to form out of the mud, just as every plant that has life needs water to grow. That is why the Flood story represents the water that filled the earth and soaked the ground so soft that Spiritual man grew out like a seed that rots under the ground first before germinating in the place.

Therefore, our Souls are under the ground like the "semend/soul" of a plant that remains under the soil to hold up that plant.

The word 'Semend' is a new word that the Spirit put on my tongue to explain the spiritual part (soul) of a plant that is not seen by our eyes but is present and possesses all that the plant needs to bear stems, leaves, and fruits.

Inside the semend are all the properties of a plant stored to be supplied to it according to their various timing; the stem grows at its appointed time, the leaf comes out at its own time, and all other things follow in their time.

In the same way as a plant, so is the Soul of a man planted into the soil through which the Spirits manifest unto us. The Soul elongates and is present in us as the spiritual part of this human frame. It serves as the pivot point on which human beings move.

First End of our world

Our world shall end with "Fire". The word 'Fire' is the spiritual meaning of the kind of destruction human science shall cause to this world.

Whatever threat any country poses to another should never be taken lightly because they are slowly and secretly building and piling up dangerous weapons of mass destruction.

While superpower countries are busy suppressing other nations from acquiring dangerous weapons, behold, they're developing more new dangerous weapons every day because they want to maintain their superpower roles.

When the right time comes, the entire human race shall desire war having been sick and tired of disgrace by other powers.

On the other hand, those with superpowers would not hold back from using all their ballistic missiles and firebombs, along with their chemical bombs.

The entire human race shall enter a world war that will dry waters and burn the trees so bad that people will die of hunger and thirst.

There will be diseases [emanating from those chemicals], and people will choose to commit suicide rather than live and suffer.

This will mark the end of the human race but not the foreclosure until the rapture comes.

Second end of our world

God's cycle of destruction and recreation of the world (Rapture-Resurrection-Judgment&New World)

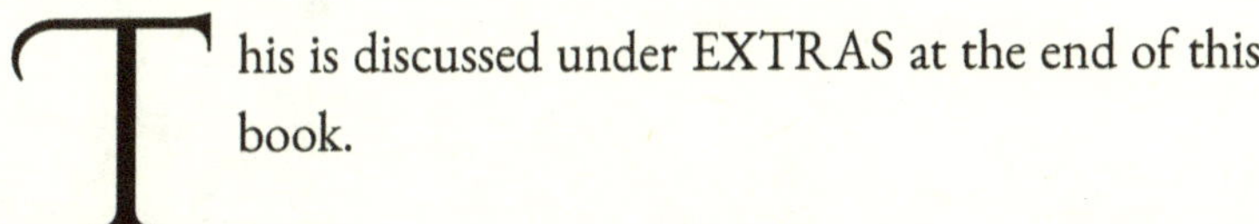

This is discussed under EXTRAS at the end of this book.

Part Two

The Simplification of Creation

The whole story about the making of man

Satan is very significant in the story I'm going to tell you about the Human Race and what happened to white and black men in Heavens (in the first and unseen world), which has been taking its toll on us in the second world. This explains how Satan broke away from God, their King (President if you like), and he became a second king (Another President) using the same knowledge of God to do things his own way.

Talking about human creation, the Bible gave us a glimpse of how the black man came about in the story of Noah's three children after Adam & Eve, who were earlier depicted in the Bible as white or whatever color Bible men gave them. But there is more to this creation system that man is yet to find out in part II of this book under the heading-*Forming of physical man.*

But before we go there, let's see how the Bible writers

tabulated the generations of the first human and his wife (Adam and Eve) and their descendants before the other man (Noah), whom they said gave birth to all humans in this big world of different races [human colors].

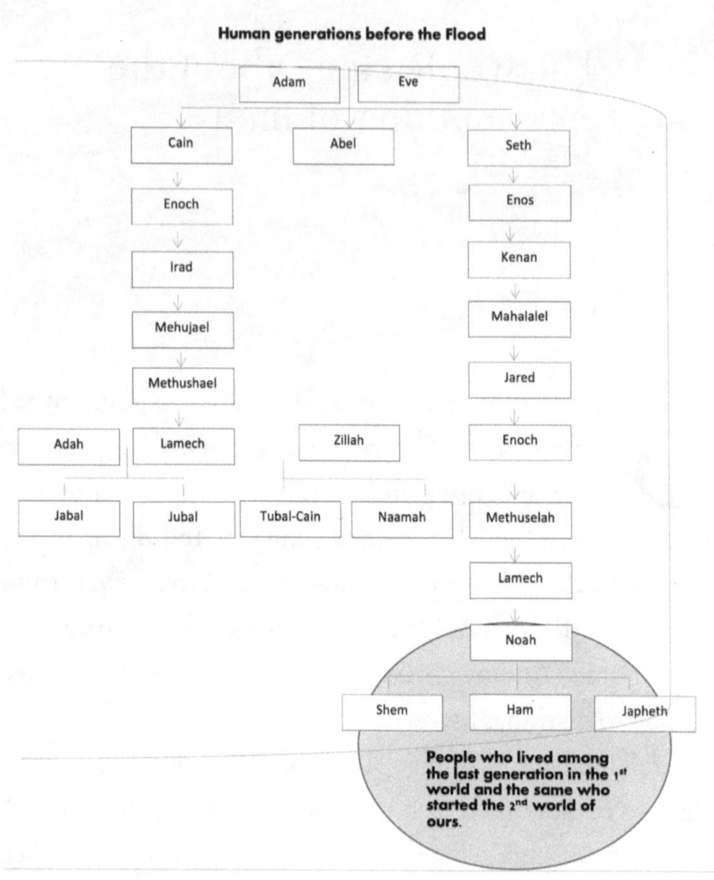

Sadly enough, the table above [primarily] contains God's allegorical depictions of Spiritual existences. They're the spiritual roots (souls) culminating in physical humans in the Middle East, where God planned [in the Spirit Realm] to descend one day to begin interacting with mankind. We discussed this group in part one as the pre-earth generations, from the Garden to the Flood. We provided you with many scriptures and historical facts for your convenience.

We told you that Noah and his family are the new human generation [physical humans], whom historians or anthropologists called the "Early Men" who started our world system after the Flood. We said they existed in the first world before it was destroyed. We said one of them (Noah) obtained great knowledge of construction when he built the Ark in the first world.

We said Noah and his family possessed different characteristics during the First World when they knew science to make tools and implements and to build houses. Still, when the Flood occurred [transition period], they were transformed into different beings, and as such, they had a new beginning, so they didn't know science anymore to build houses or farms.

Their lack of scientific knowledge (creating things) became the reason why early men are reported to have lived in natural caves and hollows of wood, strangulated animals with their bare hands for food, and had no idea for farming until their offsprings later received the knowledge of making things that enabled them to dig better caves for themselves then later learned how to build houses. Their children who came after them many thousands of years later have been discussed in the Bible and tabulated [accordingly] as seen below.

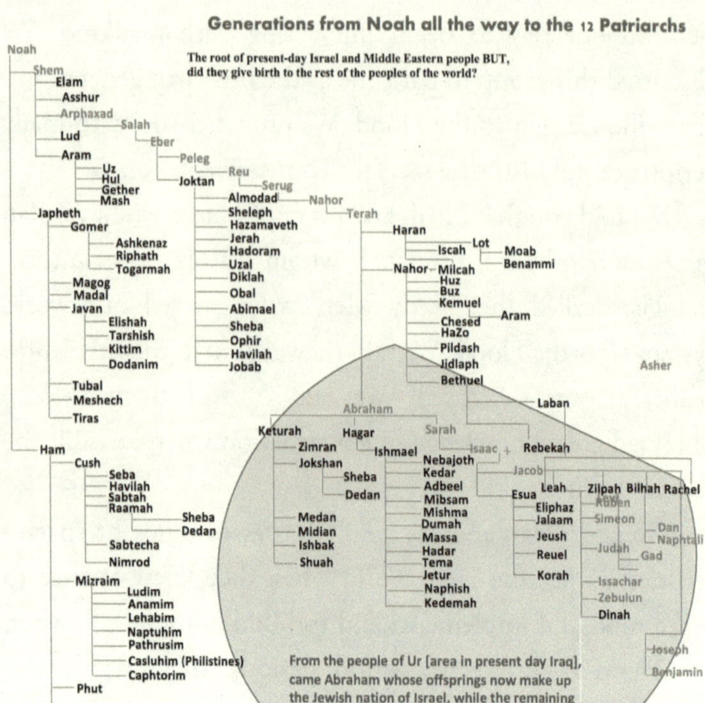

By definition of the chart depicting Noah and the 12 great generations [Noah and his sons {Shem, Japheth, and Ham}] + their children + grandchildren + great grandchildren + great, great-grandchildren and on, and on until present day people; it is easy to recognize them [they all share similar resemblance {facial and cultural}] consistently to prove that the Bible has only accounted for a little fraction of the world's entire human population that makes up different types of peoples.

That's why this book says [we], the generation that lives by this year 2018, are the direct product of all the people who came out of the mud after the biblical "Flood" subsided. Among them, a man named Noah was chosen as a symbol of human beginnings on earth. He (Noah) was just a sample of how all the spiritual people came into being physical people by their races (colors) and languages they developed in the Spirit Realm.

To prove that there were different humans on this planet, apart from the people of the Middle East, the generations of Noah's children started meeting other people while they were spreading out. That's why anthropologists would describe different civilizations around the world just within the same period civilization was going on in the Mesopotamia region (Middle Eastern region of the planet.) Because they met the black humans in Africa, they could not go down the land to occupy the entire Central, West, East, and South Africa; instead, they got stuck in the Northern part of Africa since it borders the Middle East.

This storytelling of man's spirituality and physicality [juxtaposing two events] started when the Spirit of God came to earth to begin His direct interaction with physical mankind. To do so, He first landed in a particular place [now called "Middle East"] where He introduced Himself to humankind. He then chose a specific people as His earthly family [to use] to start His reaching out to the entire world, and that brought in the people of Ur, from whom the story of Abraham is told to include the nation Israel today that is the birthplace of our Lord Jesus.

Unfortunately, the people who left Ur [now Israelis {Jews}] interpreted God's choice of them as the first human family to be that God was for them alone. That's how they adopted the word "Gentile" to mean "non-Jewish or unclean people who God doesn't want." And until God told them [Jews] through one of their own [Peter] that the Gentiles belonged to Him as well, they (Jews) believed that they were the only people belonging to this Almighty God.

Arguments about black ancestry

The early interpreters of the Christian book surely didn't understand the allegory in Genesis concerning the evolution [the coming into this world] of the black race, as the genealogy of Adam and Eve or Noah and family shows that only the lineages of Shem, Japheth, and Ham, all bearing the same features of the Jews and Arabs, make up the peoples of the Bible.

However, it seems that by the time Jewish historians began to compile all the pieces of their histories together, they had discovered that there was another color of people living on another land now called "Africa," so they had to attribute the origination of blacks to the darker son "Ham" of Noah.

It is against this human error [Not God's error] that the Almighty God has raised me to make clear that the three colors [Fair, dusky, and dark] of Noah's children remain the same among the Asiatic people of today and as such the assertion about Ham's descendants in the early Gojjam Kingdom, now Ethiopia, is the one that gave birth to an entirely new race called the Black Race is untrue.

Several factors must be examined to disprove this old theory [I repeat; human interpretational error, not God's error], beginning with the physical features of the darker people of Asia who are now living in Ethiopia in Africa, which do not actually conform to the features of the Blacks who are located below the north of Africa.

The voice told me that the darker skin scenario in the story of Ham remains symbolic of what every race experiences internally. We can still see even in this modern time with some Indians (Indians in Asia) who have very dark (black) colored people among them. Will that make dark Indians descendants of black Africans? NO!!! This is the same as when you look at some Ethiopians and others who have some dark-colored people. This does not still make them black Africans. The same variations in the color system also affect those we call "white people" in this modern world who do have sparkling white and lower white people among them, and even in the coloration of their eyes.

So, the three colors described in the Bible under Noah's three sons, Japheth (fair), Shem (dusky), and Ham (darker), while they were yet in the first world represent the three primary human colors (white, semi-white and black) that evolved [came] out of the soil/mud during the period of the Flood and have thus become the physical humans in the second world [you may continue to the heading that says- *Forming of Physical man*].

Crossbreeding in the Spirit realm

The condition of different coloration in a specific race, as we see around the world, is a perfect symbol of the crossbreeding system that occurs in the Spirit Realm. It is the symbolism of why and how we find some sparkling white-skinned people and lower white-skinned people, why and how some white people possess black or brown coloration around the pupil of the eyes, why and how some Jews, Arabs, Asiatic Indians, Ethiopians, and others of Asia may have dark skin, why and how some other white people and dusky people possess short or long hair plants, why and how some black Africans possess light skin so much so that they may be seen as white looking in a distance while most black Africans are brown-skinned and few are very charred [they get as black as carbon], and why and how every race of a people have some short and tall elements.

All of these natural occurrences apply to all peoples

regardless of their race, and that explains why Ethiopians who live below the northern part of the Island of Africa are not of black African descent.

But this book doesn't disprove Arab-looking Ethiopians to be the descendants of Noah's son, Ham, as in (Gen. 10:6 NIV), for they share the same ancestry, culture, religion, and body features with the Arabs of Asia. To be emphatic, they indeed migrated from the Middle East to a new place across the Red Sea and have no connection to black origin!

Spiritual man and physical man (The souls)

Now, let's find out how every human being [physical human] came into this world, but before we get there, let's start with the meanings of the three different Bible verses that talk about the creation of the male and the female. The first male and female God created in Gen. 1:27 are the souls of both man and woman that exist in Heaven with God right by His Throne. In architectural terms, this will be the first design [call it a blueprint/model] of both man and woman that stands for the way physical man shall be. Still, in technological terms, they represent remote controls God uses to manipulate the physical humans on earth.

So, after God had made these sketches, He created two other copies (duplicated souls) in Gen. 2:7 and 2:22 out of the originals, and He called them man and woman. Later, these are the second souls [Metonymy] that shall be inserted in a frame called the "Body," and God shall say He created them out of the dust.

So, why did God make two different Souls for the man and the woman? Firstly, in the simplest way, God uses the original Souls as communication tools [as in science, like remote controls] to control/manipulate humans in The way He likes. Secondly, in the most complex way, God's Throne (Heaven above) is His Main Station, so the original Souls stand for Main Towers while the duplicated Souls now covered with human flesh stand for Antennas to receive and send signals from and to God.

If this is hard to understand, then study how and why communication science on earth made the Main Tower Station different from where all signals are sent/transmitted [a local area where Antennas/terminals are planted to receive and send back signals to Main Tower Station].

I urge you to study the science of communication systems in our world. You will find out that our voices and images are all processed in the Main Station no matter how far it is, so there is this back-and-forth movement between the Tower and the terminal (between a central point and a sub-point). This science of technology on earth today simplifies why and how God made two human Souls that appear in the Christian book of the Bible, but the prophets and apostles to whom God gave this information did not have the authority of interpretation conferred on me (Paul – the storyteller) today by the Spirit of God. Their work was primarily limited to writing the messages, so they didn't make things as straightforward as I was told to do.

In scriptures like: "And the multitude of them that

believed were of one heart and of one **soul**, and ..." (Act. 4:32 KJV), and "Now my **soul** is troubled, and what shall I say?' 'Father..." (Joh. 12:27 NIV); the "soul" is considered a part of the body as the life-giving part to the flesh. The soul is, therefore, personalized as something that feels with the flesh. Still, its literal meaning is found in other scriptures like Matt. 10:28 NIV that says: "Do not be afraid of those who kill the body but cannot kill the **soul**," Revelation 6:9-11 NIV says: Verse 9, " When he opened the fifth seal, I saw under the altar the **souls** of those who had been slain because of the word of God and the testimony they had maintained." Verse 10, "They called out in a loud voice, " 'How long, Sovereign Lord, holy and true, until you judge the inhabitants of the earth and avenge our blood?' " Verse 11, "Then each of them was given a white robe, and they were told to wait a little longer, until the full number of their fellow servants, their brothers and sisters, were killed just as they had been," and including Eccl. 12:7 KJV which says: "Then shall the dust return to the earth as it was: and the Spirit shall return unto God who gave it." These scriptures confirm Gen. 2:7 NIV: Verse 7, "Then the Lord God formed a man from the dust of the ground and breathed into his nostrils the breath of life, and the man became a living being." In KJV translations, it says: "The man became a living soul."

Thus, the man who became a living being/soul here refers to the Spiritual human (Soul) who has now been covered with the mud of the earth. [In this book, I have shown an image depicting how the Spiritual man came out of the ground with mud covering him].

These two types of soul (Gen. 2:7 and 2:22) are the

driving forces to the frames of the two human bodies [the engines powering the bodies]: the male and female bodies. They're the ones that are immortal (Matt. 10:28 KJV, Rev. 6:9-11 KJV, and Eccl. 12:7 KJV) and are those which the Spirits of God (Angels) come for when a man/woman dies.

They're the ones that shall represent a man or a woman to face judgment in Heaven, (Rev. 6:9 KJV) after a man/woman dies because they're spirits. They're the ones that move about in the Spirit Realm while a man/woman is asleep, and when he/she gets up the next day, he/she says he/she has had a dream. They're the ones that act like a man/woman that encounters the Spirit world because they're the Spirit parts of the human body: Verse 23, "May God himself, the God of peace, sanctify you through and through. May your whole **spirit**, soul and body be kept blameless at the coming of our Lord Jesus Christ" (Thess. 5:23 NIV).

Difficulty in Bible understanding

The reason why Christians find it difficult to understand Bible scriptures like the ones mentioned above, which led to Christian divides, as well as different denominational beliefs in the world today, is that these various scriptures that were given were scattered throughout the Bible by the prophets and apostles who were not gifted to the interpretation of the Spirit but were only called to bring God closer to mankind and to write the messages of God.

But what is accurate and yet confusing to the human mind that I'm called to vivify had been revealed long ago in the doctrines of the Latter Days Saints.

Therefore, I implore you to allow me to inject this piece of information here again before I can give you clarity on the three parts of man.

In their book, they have a topic, *"Where did I come from?*, which is on page 2 of their Tract that has the title

"The Plan of Salvation." So, it is written therein, *"Your life didn't begin at birth, nor will it end at death. You are made up of a spirit body (sometimes called the soul) and a physical body. Your Heavenly Father created your spirit, and you lived with Him as a spirit before you were born on earth. You knew and loved Him, and He knew and loved you. This period is called pre-earth life"*.

This is part of the teachings of the Latter Days Saints, which I haven't seen with any other church's teaching to come so close to this truth of man's spiritual existence in the Heavens before becoming physical.

This report is important today because it lays the ground for what has been fully disclosed to me for all the peoples of the earth to understand the works of their God.

Clarity on the three parts of human

The human body, as in three parts, functions differently: (1) As a spirit, it has the ability to fly to different locations to see different things and places [at this time, the name of the soul changes to a different word as "spirit" just as the name of stilt water changes to be "Vapor" when it begins to fly into the air as gas]. This happens to enable the soul to interact with the Spirit world where it sometimes receives attacks and fights wars and, or gets defeated or wins wars while physical man is asleep; (2) As a soul, the soul remains in the body to keep it alive [at this time it acts like stilt water that gives out vapor while it remains in place for human and animal uses], and (3) As a body/flesh it continues to receive life from the soul so that blood circulation, repairs, and other things going on in the body system.

In most cases, when a physical human gets out of sleep with a fever or in a bad mood, it is the human soul/spirit that was attacked last night, but all of what happened to it has been communicated to the physical body of the man or woman.

Mechanically, the "soul" + flesh + bones + veins + water and all others are put together to be called "human beings." This is the same as a tiny engine (driving force) + all the metals + water + wires + rubbers + oil, and all others are combined to be called a "vehicle."

Let's say the second soul that lives in the human body functions as a conduit/medium of transmission and receiving. That's why every spirit enters the human body through the soul. The soul connects human beings to Heaven, as the electric wire connects two terminal points to each other.

The complexity of the soul is expressed throughout the Christian book in different verses, so much so that the human mind gets confused over its real meaning. That's why different denominations have different understandings of it while downplaying some aspects of it.

Human creation (how the three colors were formed)

Human science in well-developed countries today is a little more than half equal to science in the Heavens. Did I say it right? Maybe I should say the science on earth in well-developed countries is just 56% of how much science in Heavens is at the time of this manuscript [2018]. This is to further say that before man knew science on earth, science was at its advanced stage in Heaven already.

Therefore, the machine used to make human beings in Heaven was laid out in three separate layers. From the first layer, the **white man** came out. From the second layer, the **semi-white man** came out, and from the third layer, the **black man** came out [Allegory].

That was a scientific process in Heaven at the time, but that could only be understood now from the human science point of separating a mixture on earth, particularly the mixture of crude oil.

Similarly, another creation ["So, God created man in His own image, in the image of God created He him; male and female created He them." {Gen.1:27}] incorporates how He (God) created both male and female together, but the scientific process [unexplained part of God in the Jewish book] was done in succession. Thus, the male was made first and he was called "son" which means "second" after the first image of God, then the female followed and was called "daughter" which means "daughsterestiky" [it is a Spiritual word that described a completely new creature/creation out of the second creation for the purpose of doing things that the son is not to do].

Analogy of Fractional Distillation

Scientists use a means called "Fractional Distillation" to separate crude oil. The process is conducted by heating crude oil [mixture of hydrocarbon] as high as 600 degrees Celsius, and the mixture boils to form vapor (gases). When a substance in the vapor reaches a height where the temperature of the column is equal to that substance's boiling point, it will **condense** to form a liquid. The substance with the lowest boiling point will condense at the highest point in the column; substances with higher boiling points will condense lower in the column.

Gasoline (Petrol) is a top product on the column that comes out at 150 degrees Celsius, but I want to focus this discussion on white and black substances found in the mixture of crude oil. They're called "Paraffin Wax" and "Asphalt/Bitumen" as two of the products that can be obtained from the bottom most (residual) products when they're heated at 400 degrees Celsius.

"Paraffin Wax" as a white substance is used in making candles while "Asphalt" as a thick black substance is often used in road pavement.

Surely, this seems very weird, but following this process explains exactly how three major colors; white, semi-white, and black were produced in Heaven by way of heavenly science in the creation of human beings.

Perhaps one theologian may ask; so why man was not put in three colors in the beginning, but it came after Adam and Eve began to populate the earth? Well, the answer is; God uses symbolism/allegory to explain Spirituality in connection to physicality. That means, even though everything happened from the beginning but the entire story of one man (Adam) having many children who in turn had their own children and the process continued till his generation filled the earth was a representation of what physical men were yet to go through in their own households. This explains how a single man in our today world often give birth to several children (maybe 10 boys + 4 girls),

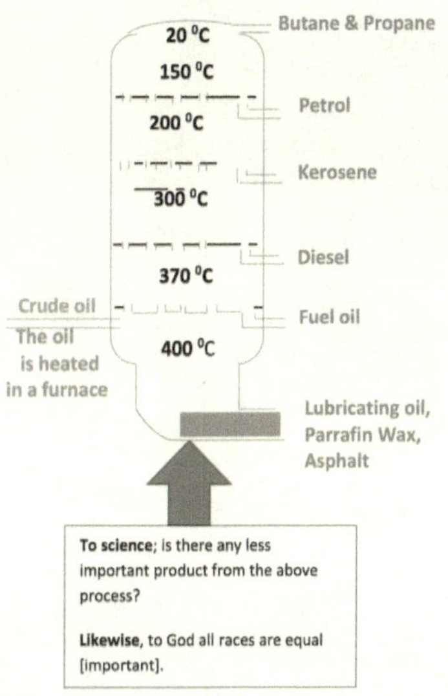

who, in turn, may give birth to different numbers of children while their children may give birth to other children so that their generations unarguably become uncountable over many centuries. In fact, some of his children may not be able to see or know their relations around the world.

So, in the same manner, as using one man, Adam, to allegorize the process of Spiritual man's population, Noah's three sons were used to allegorize races (very, very distinct humankind).

Forming of physical man

I hope we understand that God has made us know where the Garden of Eden is through Ezek. 28:13-17 since Moses was not clear enough to tell his people that the picture he drew in Genesis, which he called the "Garden of Eden," was something he saw in the Spirit Realm, like a heavenly Jerusalem. So, IF we understand this, we can move forward to understand that all the depictions in the Garden are Spiritual characters that an architect [God] put in place before forming all physical things.

Therefore, when the time came for the Spirit of God to move [sprinkle the seeds of all human colors] on the face of the earth to form the physical man out of the soil He had made, He poured down water from heaven to fill every corner of the earth to soften the ground.

While the ground remained soaked with water, the spirits of mech-anics came down and moved all over the earth to sprinkle the seeds of three human colors. After that, humankind began to form out of the soil just like a plant sprouts out of the ground. In this way, every human type [clean color (white), half-clean color (semi-white), and dark color (black)] residing in the Spirit realm was formed out of the earth in different parts of the world. They germinated out of the ground one by one, just like plant seeds shoot out of the soil one by one after they've been sown into the soil.

Black race as distinct

Therefore, the two-word term "Black Race" refers to a special group of humankind whose intelligence is different from that of the rest of the world.

This brings us to how the spirit discusses intelligence with me, but before that, let's see how the world sees intelligence: **Intelligence** [among several definitions] is a mental ability involved in reasoning, perceiving relationships and analogies, calculating, and learning quickly. Others say it is a hypothetical idea that they have defined as being reflected by certain types of behavior.

But the spirit tells me it is the *science* [knowledge] of creation of knowing right and wrong, whereby one ceaselessly seeks to find alternative means to better everything in life all the time.

This means that *intelligence* is not just any kind of knowledge or common sense of knowing things; it embodies action to improve one's life condition. It doesn't support complacency or stagnation.

Indeed, this definition seems to embrace one and oppose one of two available definitions: Einstein said, "The true sign of **intelligence** is not knowledge but imagination." Socrates said, "I know that I am intelligent, because I know that I know nothing."

Here, Einstein does not evade knowledge; instead, he encourages thinking that drives everyone to action. So, by way of imagination (the act of thinking tirelessly), a man brings about change while accepting that you know nothing truly confirms your complacency in doing new things.

Let's carefully look at the definition of Intelligence given to me again: The spirit used the word <u>*science*</u> to define intelligence, so since science is a word denoting creativity, THEN Intelligence is a technical knowledge that embodies logical reasoning for creative arts that shape the look of the world to a comfortable environment but not how to do other non-creative activities such as to perceive [*the ability to see, hear, or become aware of something through the senses {the same kind of ability every insane person also has to be able to flee dangerous scenes}*].

So, let me ask this question: Why do people come to the Western world if not for the things [infrastructural developments] made possible by the science of technology? [So, you see, technology means 'technical knowledge or technical study and it comes from the white man].

So, when Socrates says he knows that he knows nothing, he is actually referring to common knowledge/sense that the insane man has to use to pick foods to eat [not intelligence] because he knows that food is needed for survival, yet he's not as good as one of us.

So, let's see how intelligence has shaped the look of this world by asking you this second question: If men of knowledge (intelligence) had not been thinking and thinking over the period mankind has been in existence, where would the world have been now? I'm sure you will agree that the world would have been poorer and underdeveloped without information technology, electricity, heavy equipment, airplanes, cars, road pavement, etc, even while we still have new songs and dances in our various villages. In fact, I have been thinking that without the plane, I may have never come to America in this part of the world to see the ways of the white people here.

Therefore, since the black race has not come to know technical things by themselves [except by learning], they are [regardless of where they are found around the world] vividly different from the Ethiopians, who are part of the semi-white race (dark Middle Easterners).

Apart from their level of intelligence, Black Africans are distinguishable because of the difference in their hair textures and hairstyles from the Arab-looking Ethiopians and the rest of the world, in comparison to their cultures and traditions to the Arabian Ethiopians and the rest of the world, and in comparison to their facial looks.

[Please let me inject this as a reminder of what was opaquely written earlier in another section, and that is to say, the whites always guide blacks, and as such, the blacks tend to improve their system of life by emulation. If this were not so, then Africans would have developed far beyond where they are now in their places, all by themselves.

This is why this book stands to fill the gap that exists here. It is the very reason why God spoke to me to tell the entire story concerning human creation without altering the Bible story of Adam and Eve.

The beginning of physical science (Human science)

When this first group of men was formed, they had no knowledge of making things. They started with no scientific knowledge until a particular generation began to receive information from the forces of the Spirit world about what to do and how to do it.

This process of receiving instructions from unseen forces continues with scientists who invent things. Early scientists may hear voices, see things in space that no one else could see, or even dream dreams to do certain things. This is what happened to them while they were laying the foundations for what modern scientists follow now, and it is the same pattern that occurred to me from 2006 to mid-2008 when I heard voices that explained everything that I was commanded to write in different books in our time.

That process of making things into physical forms is now

referred to as human science. It has grown into many phases from generation to generation and is now at its highest peak, called "Technology."

Allegory of shipbuilding

The Bible's story of the Flood is a parable (Allegory) of the end of a world in which the Soul was prepared to come to live on physical earth.

The Flood period is like the gestation period today when a spiritually made human being has to wait for a particular time to be born into the physical world.

The building of an "Ark" became a symbol of a time in the life of the last days' generation of physical man when science would reach its highest peak of building a large ship called an "Aircraft carrier." The Aircraft carrier would be a huge ship that will have the capacity to carry any size of animals, a large number of foodstuffs, a large number of people, every type of vehicle regardless of size, and a flying machine that may be sent out into the land to take pictures and record information to bring back to the ship.

The flying machines would be used to travel to the land and collect food to bring on board to feed the crew.

Therefore, whatever boat archeologists claim today to prove the physical existence of the Ark of Noah is a fossil of an old boat that once existed after Noah and his people left this world.

People are building models simply by following the description Moses made in Genesis. Those kinds of objects must be verified now in this millennium. So, I want to use this book as a wake-up call to all Bible scholars to do the same as in 2018 on the *16 fragments of the Dead Sea Scrolls* from the Bible Museum owned by the Evangelical Christian and Billionaire Steve Green in Washington, DC. The report said the 16 fragments were sent to Germany to verify the authenticity of the rare biblical artifacts, and, of course, the result proved otherwise that they had characteristics inconsistent with ancient origin.

In this Ark case, we're to search for evidence consistent with early man's life; what the first man, supposedly Noah and his family, had in terms of tools and what he did in terms of construction skills after the Flood then parallel those information with the stages of development that mankind has been going through until the time of man having the first knowledge of building a tall building as well as through the time that brought us to building boats and large ships capable of carrying heavy load of several planes and war tanks.

One thing that I know for sure is that every race started small before it got bigger, as it may be today.

Early Jews made assumptions

Early Jews made assumptions about the Garden due to physical landmarks.

The contemporary men of Moses knew the land features of what was then known as the Mesopotamia region, which we know today as the Middle Eastern region. So, when Moses drew the greenness of the Garden with trees, animals, rivers, and minerals with names that still exist today in the Middle East, it was easy for them to view the Garden as being on earth.

But after living with that assumption for so many years, God then revealed the true location of the Garden to a man named Ezekiel during the tyrannical reign of the King of a place called "Tyre" on earth.

Let's take a brief look at Ezekiel 28:13-17 again, where it's written that [verse13] Satan was in Eden, the garden of God; [verse14b-15] perfect and sinless until he did sin, and God said,

17[b] "So I threw you to the earth" NIV [Satan is being thrown down here in this verse 17b].

The focus point is the phrase "*threw to the earth*" to see that the Garden is in a different location where Lucifer (now Satan) rebelled. Then, he was sent out from that location to another location where God made a spectacle of him. Now, God revealed to me that the Garden of Eden is an Allegory.

The Spirit of God, who brought this message to me in 2008, further explains how we should reconcile the difference in men's assumptions due to their lack of Spiritual understanding and the truth in the Bible.

By this, the man said to me there are places and things in Heavens used in the Bible as symbols (Allegories) for the same names that we have on earth, and he then gave me a comparison between Apostle John and Prophet Moses:

Comparison of Apostle John and Prophet Moses

John	Moses
In John's case, he made it clear that he was caught up in the Spirit while he was on the Island of Patmos. Because of John's clarity in his writing, everything he saw and wrote about became very clearly referred to as Spirituality (Spiritual images and events). In John's story, he saw a city called "Jerusalem" yet to come on earth, different Churches (different behaviors of church people) now reflecting our behaviors today, and different manifestations of Satan on earth that we can see today. Because of the way John described the scene in which he encountered God on the Island, it made it easier for the people of his time to distinguish the Jerusalem in Heaven (Rev. 21:2 and 10) from the Jerusalem on earth (2 Chron. 6:5-6). It also made it easier for his contemporary kinsmen to accept that everything he said he saw was nothing about Physicality but purely Spirituality. This made using "Allegory" in the Book of Revelation easier to understand. Similarly, names of persons, things, places, and events exist in Heaven as they also exist on earth but have not been revealed at all or at the same time in one particular book of the Bible.	In Moses' case, he didn't make it clear that he was caught up in the Spirit while he was on the top of Mount Sanai. Moses didn't tell his people that most of the 40 days and 40 nights he spent on Mt. Sanai were spent in Heaven when he went into trance. And while his spirit was caught up in Heaven, the heavenly dwellers (angels) took him on a tour where he saw the different parts of Heaven. Because Moses didn't provide his exact state of affairs after he saw the "Burning Bush," it became difficult for those who picked up the writings he left behind to know if he was depicting Spiritual images. They didn't know if what the angels had shown him as the "Garden of Eden" was just the blueprint (like in architectural design) of what God had purposed to be the earth, and everything depicted in it was just a picture of how things would look on earth. They didn't know that the names of the Rivers like Euphrates, Tigris, Nile, and the region of Mesopotamia that they had already known on earth also exist in heaven, as John told us about the existence of a heavenly Jerusalem. Because Moses didn't make his situation straightforward on Sanai, mankind today has not recognized the similarity between the "Eden, the garden" of God in Ezekiel 28:13 and the "Garden of Eden" in Genesis. **Note:** The water above the Firmament (Gen. 1:6-8) also has names in the Heavens similar to ours on earth because the earth is just a replica of the Heavens.

He said those mistakes in the Bible were not made by God but by the man who didn't properly understand the several parables (Tales) that came from God.

Racial disparity (Science favored one)

This is another tale. There was one guy dearly loved by his father. [In this story alone, he may be called the eldest child who was always there to entertain his father.] When the youngest child was always there to run errands for their father, then call both of them the first two sons of their father.

The father loved his eldest son so much that He taught him not music alone but almost everything that the father knew. The eldest son grew very proud of himself for the level of knowledge he had acquired from his father, so he began to do things he was not instructed or allowed to do.

Every time he broke some laws, his father would only reprimand him. The father loved him so much that it became difficult for Him to decide what kind of punishment to give the son under the heavenly laws. But one day, the eldest son messed with the nursery [the "Nursery" is the Garden of

Eden, as we have discussed already], and his action went too far with the father.

Therefore, the father cast him away (drove/rejected him), brought the youngest son closer to Himself, and said to the youngest son, "You are my heart; please don't disappoint me too."

When this happened, the eldest son turned violent against his father; he destroyed things everywhere so that the father sent an army unto him, but he knew so much like his father that he fled from his father's house ["house" here means main dwelling place] and went to another side of the unseen world. He named his place "Aquebus" – meaning "This is my own living place or leave me; I'll live here."

From Aquebus, he launched a war (a rebellion) against his father, but it was actually not to remove his father because he knew he couldn't do so; rather, he was fighting to remove his youngest brother so that he could return to his place.

Because of his popularity, he had many friends and admirers. Some of these people went with him and fought with him, but they didn't win the war. Instead, they fled from the upper part of the Spirit world [let's say it was the developed part of Heavens at the time], and they went down to another part of the Spirit world [say the underdeveloped part of Heavens at the time] and they formed their own country where they made their own rules.

Some of their rules followed the organic rules, but most of the organic rules were either altered or modified.

One of such altered rules was how to dispense science to mankind (the sequence of how to create things) since their

Great King (the Father—God) chose to abandon man, thus leaving him in the care of the wayward son.

This is the fall of Satan from Heaven that is stated in Rev. 12:7-8 and Ezk. 28:13 & 17.

Why does God leave us infected?

Heavenly stories have become very, very old, and the revised system after the rebellion took place is what constitutes the word of God today. In the revised version of the system of things in Heaven, God chose Jesus as His First and Beloved. At the same time, Lucifer lost his respect as the Beloved and his authority as the eldest in the sight of his father, God, and therefore became known as Satan, pronounced "Sat-an," which means "Turn Against" or "Turn against Constituted Laws."

Let's consider the removal of Lucifer in the first place to be like cutting the first large branch of a tree because it is infected to choose the second and best-looking branch to be the first from there on.

Because he caused his father so much grief and weeping over his departure, in the mind of God, he is considered a dead child who shouldn't be counted among the living, and that makes Jesus the first among the children of God as is written in the Bible and so shall it be forever.

Satan, as the original first son, was taught almost everything that the Father knows, and that gives him so much strength to fight Jesus to the point of defeat unless God intervenes by sending additional power to Jesus.

The reality is that Satan has almost an equal power that makes it difficult for God to break every satanic infliction on man. Instead, God would rather choose to let the condition stay with the person even while He (God) has a piece of work for the person to do for Him (God.)

It was under such conditions as "Leave it and let it be" that God could not heal Moses from stammering when Moses complained that he could not go to Egypt because he lacked better speech. [Stammering is not a condition from God; it's a satanic affliction, and that was done on Moses by the wicked forces even before he was born because they had known his authority in the Spirit realm before he was conceived. It was their way of causing him difficulty in his lifetime].

I have a tree and a bush run analogy God gave me to explain this condition: "Leave it and let it be." When I have funds available one day to do so, I shall have a video clip of a tree that has been engulfed by a very stubborn bush run, so much so that the run enters into the tree and grows with it so that when you stand in the distance, you would imagine that the run is one of the branches of the tree. You may think that its leaves are the leaves of the tree.

God said here that this kind of entanglement makes removing the run from the tree impossible, but if you insist on doing so, you will have to hew down both the tree and the run. He advised, "Therefore leave both of them to grow together while you continue your harvest on the tree ['your harvest is the way to say continue making use of the tree even while it remains entangled by the bush run'"].

But in place of healing Moses, God gave him Aaron to be his spokesman. The example of Moses's case while God used him still exists today when we see a very strong person of God exhibiting the same old way he/she had before he/she came to Christ.

Some of these old ways include sexual immorality/promiscuity, greed for money, lies, anger, pride, etc. Now, these satanic behaviors often lead most people to ministerial failures and other catastrophes on the part of those who are not able to find a strategy to avert a cycle of such ungodly acts.

It is sad that these people of God may keep going to Church and holding their positions on earth, whether as pastors or deacons or choirs, but they're already guilty under the lower court of four judges. Some may be saved only based on God's discretion during judgment time after they may have been referred to the higher court of two, Jesus and his Father God. [To learn more about heavenly judgment, go down to the EXTRAS in this book.]

Parallelism of healing and infliction

Now, the city of Aquebus was completed as the headquarters, and Satan became their official ruler, who appointed leaders to take charge of the earth. They have their hierarchy arranged in the order of Satan, the King, assisted by one agent of meaningful powers, supervising four rulers of the four corners of the earth who are assisted by seven rulers of the seven continents who are also assisted by all rulers sitting in the Spirit realm as leaders of countries in the world. This is how you can keep drawing the pyramid down and down and down to a ruler over a person.

Every year, the seven rulers meet with the King, who in turn [the seven] meet with the countries, the countries meet with the regions, and so on.

This chain of power transmission shows how powers descend from heaven [this is the lower heaven where Satan and his people live] to earth and how these forces [called "gods of our lands"] fight among themselves. Their fights are what we receive in the physical form of wars that range from country-by-country down to individual quarrels and killings.

The four and seven rulers acting to assist Satan in the Spirit Realm are commonly referred to as Powers and Principalities sitting over the earth. They're Satan's chief commanders. They receive and distribute powers from Satan. They appraise, judge, and punish lower rulers of the earth. Their judgments and punishments of lower rulers are seen in the world when one power is inflicted with illness or struck down with death.

They're the reason behind power clashes around the world, which are seen in two forms: (1) in underdeveloped nations or communities, the gods that serve as powers in those areas fight and defeat one another, which is witnessed by one witchcraft disabling or killing another witchcraft or when one powerful joo-joo man (Soothsayer/Sorcerer) strikes down another joo-joo man and; (2) in developed nations where science and technology take over traditional methods, the gods become the givers of knowledge of weapons of mass destruction among nations.

In making weapons and stirring conflicts among nations, they succeed in creating the means of supplying themselves with meals by feeding on human flesh and blood.

In all this, more knowledge (science) is given to a particular sect of people in reciprocation for inflicting more injuries and deaths during battles. Although other factors are involved in the reasons for the knowledge of weapon making, any nation that kills more people is definitely appeasing the lower gods with blood sacrifice under the homage system.

They're also the dispensers of healing powers (both scientific and traditional) given to lower gods to repel attacks from other gods and repair inflicted persons in the nations and communities they control.

Dispensation of human science

At the beginning of their administration, these seven rulers met with their King (Satan) in Aquebus and deliberated regarding the use of tools (human beings are their tools to do their works and instruments to amuse themselves on earth). In that meeting, they chose to follow the sequence of the creation of man.

This means that the breakaway agent (Satan) who started to run the earth before God turned around to begin speaking to mankind was the one who chose to teach human science in the order of the three colors.

So, they (the earth's gods/spirits/forces/powers) met in the big city of Aquebus and decided that each local leader should follow the organic law (their own golden rule). By this rule, those powers that sit over each group of people (principally each color or race) must wait for instruction before imparting any physical science to that group of mankind.

They not only agreed to the principle of dispensation but

also set the timings for every work that would be done on the earth.

This explains why sufficient human science came to the white man, who took the lead in every aspect of life on earth, while the semi-white man trailed behind by receiving little and the black man received nothing at all (received nothing here means that the black race has not been able to participate in the science of technology; that's the main science for mankind).

This doesn't mean that the Black Race is not entitled to human science, but it has to wait for its time.

Now, can you see how Satan often does the same things as God but goes opposite to God's orders? Even while God knew that the white color was the first to have been made in Heaven, He (God) chose the middle color (semi-white people) to use to reveal Himself to mankind before He came to the white people and now the black people.

From the semi-white color people (Middle Easterners) came the prophets and apostles; from the white color people (Europeans) came Joseph Smith to receive the knowledge of the pre-earth man; and from the black people came Paul-the storyteller to review the works of the early ones and reveal the unveiled secrets of the Spirit world.

God used Asia to depict the earth

After we have read and understood Ezek. 28:13-17, the Garden of Eden can now be accepted as a Spiritual place and one of the spheres of the milky air called "Heavens," which means that everything that was ever ascribed to it remains a Spiritual thing, name, place, or history. That is why Noah and his family should be seen and discussed in two different manners; the first part being their spiritual forms in what the Bible called the first world, and the second part being their physical forms in the second world in which Noah was reported to have come out of the boat to start a new world that continues with us today.

But when they landed [evolved into physicality] on earth, they were found on the continent of present-day Asia.

To reveal this mystery, this book was brought to modern humans to enlighten readers on how they evolved from spiritual beings into physical beings. At the same time, other spiritual humans like them had already spread throughout the world's islands before they became physical through the allegory of the flood story.

This means that the big Island of Asia was not the only place where the human species sprouted out of the ground when the water covered the entire earth but was selected by the Spirit of God to be used for Him to come down to mankind to reveal the events of the first world and its people. However, the people of Asia were chosen as the medium through which God revealed Himself as the Highest Spirit among all. That is why the world's two highest religions, Christianity and Islam, though at war with each other, were born in the place called Asia.

The fact that all the Islands (Continents) received human germination almost simultaneously when the Flood had subsided is the very reason that the Asians could meet other people in other places when they began to travel outside their original places. That's how they traded with different people and fought wars with them.

Their search for plains along larger rivers to grow food made some of them cross into the northern part of the continent of Africa. The crossing of the Asians into Africa also applied to those who occupied the area called Ethiopia, which Bible writers referred to as the "Cush" in the book of Genesis. [Technically, Cush should not be in Africa since those in Ethiopia came from Asia, where the land of Cush for the dark Asians should be sought].

Hear this: One time, I was doing research on the color of Ethiopians, and I came across what one professor from Uppsala University wrote:

"The Ethiopians are not black. Just look at their nose!"

and he continued,

"If you look in a dictionary from the 1950, you are likely to see a map of race- distribution, and there, all of Africa's Horn will be marked as Semitic people.

This is indicating that Jews, Arabs, and Ethiopians are one race. Negroes are considered another race",

he wrote.

But in the case of Negroes being another race, I (PAUL) personally object to that assertion, instead telling you that they're the same African black race and they shall remain so forever. [Emphasis] Whether there are black Israelis or American negroes, they all have their ancestral roots in Africa. Instead, they became Israelis through intermarriages in Egypt and the ancient Gojjam kingdom (present-day Ethiopia) or Americans through the slave trade.

Let's look around the world. God placed a unique group of people in specific places. He didn't mix people up. Thus, the European group [French, Italian, Dutch, British {American}, Portuguese, etc.] is located in one part of the world, the Chinese group [Indonesian, Philippine, Chinese {Taiwanese},

Korean, Thai, etc.] is in one part of the world, the Asiatic Indian group [Asiatic Indian, Pakistani, Afghan, etc.] is in one part, the North American Indian group [Cherokee, Sioux, Choctaw, etc.] is in one part, Southern American group [Brizilian, Argentinian, Mexican, Peruvian, etc.] is in one part, the Middle Eastern group [Arabian, Israeli, Kuwaiti, Iraqi, Iranian, Syrian, etc {those migrated to Africa in present-day Egypt, Ethiopia, Libya, Algeria, Tunisia, Morrocco}] is in one part. Likewise, the black group is a distinct human group placed on one side of the earth. So, wherever blacks are located doesn't indicate they were placed there naturally by God; rather, they were born there through intermarriage or migration.

When the spirit revealed to me the scientific process of human creation and the spread of the human races throughout the world that I have explained far above, I considered it more straightforward to understand than the descendants of Ham issue because if early man had had the ability to change forms from long nose to short nose and from dark skin to black skin, then the long nose must have been in extinction by now, or better still the children they bear now should continue to be changing into black race, while at the same time, the new man with the short nose must also have the ability to change into other forms by now. But NO, the features of every race since creation have remained the same and shall continue to be the same until the end comes.

This means there is more reason for modern man to change his/her early perception about the way black men or white men came about.

Middle East was God's Airbase for landing on the world

Because the Middle Easterners were the first people God decided to use [As the Airbase for landing and probably because they're at the center of the earth] to establish communication with physical man, they became both the allegory [symbol of the earth's features] and synecdoche [piece of the earth's population], which He used to explain human creation. That's why He revealed to Moses the features of their landscapes, the names of their cities, and their different kinds of people as they are with Him in Heaven.

He didn't have to explain every A and Z about the entire world's human population at the time since the Bible is just a summary of who and what God is.

Because He used this tiny group of human beings without talking about other people, they got to think that they were the first and only people that He (God) had made and from whom every mankind derived. No, no, no!!!; they were just a fraction of the world's people that God intended to reach out to, but He needed to start from somewhere to grow little by little to reach out to the rest of the world one at a time.

So, seeing their fellow dark people in Africa didn't mean that the Cush Moses talked about in the Hebrew book was in Africa. In contrast, the Gihon River that supposedly surrounds the Cush is nowhere to be found in Africa. That means seeing some of Ham's descendants in Africa shows how migration led them across the water that separates Africa from Asia [this is the word of the Lord].

But for whatever reasons, God chose the Middle Easterners as the first group of people to start His communication with a physical man after driving the spiritual man out of His dwelling place [the Upper Heaven], which became the same reason He gave them two different religions (Christianity and Islamism) to demonstrate deep Spirituality and deep Physicality.

That is to say that Christianity is primarily based on Spiritual activities about God, while Islamism is based mainly on Physical activities (cultural laws) about man.

This happened because the Jews had earlier refused to accept Spiritual truths revealed to them by Jesus, instead stuck to cultural lives, the lives created by the gods of their lands before God came down to them. They loved these things of the earth more than God's ordinances required them.

Does anyone remember in the Christian book that after the crucifixion of Jesus, the curtain tore open in the Temple, and at a later time, he gave the apostles (Jews) a symbol to accept the Gentiles? Those signs marked when the Spirit of God had officially left the Jews to start revealing other things to other peoples of the earth. Still, His first stop was at the doorstep of the Jews/Israelites, in the Arabian land where Angel Gabriel (Jibrīl) appeared unto a man of Saudi Arabia.

There was nothing like forming a new religion with Mohamad, but the Jews in Mecca and Medina rejected the messages Mohamad brought to them from God. They said he was a Gentile, so he was not qualified to hear the voice of "their" God. He was not competent in bringing a message to them to rebuke the things of their culture and tradition. Behold, God wanted to reveal the preservation of specific ways of life that would bring about sanity and equity among them. One such cultural practice was adultery. God wanted them to keep it since it was intended to prevent promiscuity, but He wanted both male and female violators punished, not only the female.

Are there black angels in Heaven?

The answer is a big YES.

In God's revelation to me concerning why dark-colored (black) angels were not depicted in the Bible but all seemed to be shown in half clean-colored (semi-white or Middle Eastern human color) or clean-colored (white color) angels, He said there are dark-colored (black) angels in the Heavens, but every black angel there has chosen to be white/bright looking with curly hair due to bleaching and curling sciences in Heavens. That's why every angel who brought messages to earth in the Bible days appeared brighter/lighter than black, all with long and curly hair.

When He said this, I concluded all by myself that the apostles and prophets in Bible days didn't know which angel was dark, dusky, or white as all always appeared bright/light in color, which was why no one had shown a black angel in the Bible.

Wherever or whoever shows any angel in dark/black

color means that he/she is attempting to create a balance between black and white importance because there is no darkness or blackness in the Heavens. This is the same as the late Musical icon Michael Jackson, bleaching himself white looking and curling his hair silky and long. It is the same as most African ladies bleaching white and completely altering their hairstyles to long, soft looks. To tell the truth, I sometimes get confused about whether some people I see on TV are black or white. So, the love of whiteness is Spiritual due to a sacred reason not permitted to be disclosed now.

Blacks of the earth yearn to be like blacks in Heavens

The angel of the Lord also said that on earth, black people want to be white, too, so much so that almost all of their women are bleaching their bodies and wearing long hair. Popularly black women of the earth love to be identified with the white color skin by changing their colors and their hair types, so much so that they're neglecting their own body makeup gradually to be white looking just as their spiritual representatives (their Souls) do in Heavens so that no one sees a black spirit/angel/demon in Heavens.

Imagine that everyone who once told me about Mamie Watta (a water spirit) said he/she had seen a white person. No one has ever said he/she has seen a black Mamie Watta.

I, too, have seen one before; she was white. My late wife saw her, too, as we sat together and looked in one direction. It was like someone ordered two of us to look that way simultaneously. She saw her, then asked me, saying, "P, did you see what I saw?" Then I asked her what she saw, and she told me about the white lady she saw passing right in front of us. Then I told her the same thing. That was in 2005.

Black man is a victim of circumstances

Black people are totally different from all other races in so many ways. One major one is their lack of scientific knowledge or their inability to popularize whatever knowledge they possess in arts and medicines to uplift their living standards. Their continuous dealings in the dark things [things that do not benefit the larger population of the physical man] have kept them lagging behind the rest of the world.

Everything every human being [no matter what color human being] does in this physical world has a Spiritual force behind it, which explains how Satan stands as a Force behind black's lack of courage to transition and transform his knowledge beyond the Spiritual.

Unfortunately, it's a circumstance of victimization of black color due to Satan's choice of seniority system.

Satan only chose the white color over the black for his selfish desire to divide and rule over the people of the world [it is His choice of making one group lower and one group higher to ensure that the entire world doesn't get the kind of benefits that come with having an abundance of knowledge together for the world to get all it needs).

He victimized the black people to such an extent that he kept them away from using their natural resources (Minerals) God had given them as a people to demonstrate the knowledge of physical science. As a result, they began to look up to the white man for everything they needed to make life comfortable and worth living. Unfortunately, white people don't have any idea how they became what they are and how the world was made unequal by a wicked force, resulting in some people down and some up, even in material possessions. So, when a leader wakes up one day to defame the black race, he is just ignorant of natural facts.

Are there women angels in Heavens?

The answer is another big YES.

This is a complex situation. This book starts with the issue of the location of the Garden of Eden revealed in Ezek. 28:13- 17, after it had been misunderstood in Genesis for several centuries.

The Garden from which Satan was thrown down to the earth contained a man and a woman. They bore children, boys and girls.

The second revelation about women in the Heavens is that there are both women's and men's demons in the atmosphere. These demons sometimes manifest into physicality whenever they want to be seen by physical men. That happened in 2005 when my late wife and I saw a water spirit lady who unveiled herself to us in a slow flash that faded from us as she walked past us.

So, let's learn what a demon is: A demon [Satan is the head Demon] is a breakaway character of God's first creation.

This means God's children in the Heavens are respectfully referred to as "Angels." Still, when one rebels or turns against God's ordinances in the Heavens, that one earns a dishonorable title in a short form as "Demon," expressly put as "Demonstrator."

Is this not similar to a government official with an honorable title called "Minister" but turned to be dishonorably addressed as "Rebel" when the minister launches an armed rebellion against a sitting government?

Therefore, the fact that women's demons operate in the atmosphere provides strong evidence that women exist in Heaven. My first book, *Interpretation First*, provides enough information on women in the Heavens.

Racial equity

But God, the one Creator of these three human colors, did not have any division in His mind, for He said all are equal, “All men [colors] are equal.”

This is the organic Law of the unseen world. Every heavenly citizen is bound to obey it without discrimination.

Science to Africa

This book is not a Bible, but it is difficult for me to avoid referencing the Bible since I’m talking about spiritual matters, particularly certain things mentioned in the Bible.

Several passages in the Bible describe Satan as the one controlling this present system of things; let’s see Ephesians 2:2 KJV, "prince of the power of the air", John 12:31 NKJV, "ruler of this world.” These two passages are evidence of the use of power/knowledge that Satan received from God, as in

Ezek. 28:16 NIV, "Verse16Through your Knowledge widespread trade you were filled with violence."

This kind of Spiritual knowledge actually means science or the making of things. Therefore, Satan is the one behind the science of this age. It is not different from what God's science for mankind shall be when the new world comes, but it is corruptible (wrongly used), so God MUST destroy it to replace it with the incorruptible.

According to Satan's rule concerning the dispensation of science [inspiring science generation by generation to grow it stage by stage], the white man was chosen in the Spirit realm to receive human science first. This is why we see white countries leading in technology today. After the white man, the semi-white man was chosen as the next race to receive human science, which is why the other color of people, whom the Europeans don't see as white, come second in line to have scientific knowledge in our world today.

In all their plans, the black race was also reserved for the last days to receive science. Now, the time has come for the black race (the last race) to receive science. This means that the black race is about to experience scientific inventions. In fact, it has already started receiving knowledge slowly in Africa, but black Africans need to embrace and support it for innovation purposes.

That's why one of the purposes of this book is to announce science to black Africa and to encourage black innovation.

The official start begins with me, a black man endowed with extra-terrestrial knowledge of how science works in this technological world.

Just a soliloquy of sober reflection

In my early days, when I started reading the Bible to hear the stories of how God spoke to certain people in those days, and they wrote the things we read every day in the Bible, I didn't understand exactly what the Bible referred to as inspired word from someone named "God" whom no one has ever seen.

It was too weird to me. I didn't believe that at all. I said some white guys just put some of those lies together. I didn't know what power was in the Bible.

Then, there came another time when I started to accept the Bible. However, I still found it difficult to believe that the apostles remained stubborn in their desire to preach and teach the gospel in the face of persecution.

I kept asking myself *what kept them brave.*

The answer was far from reaching me all those years. As my interest grew in the word, one day, I took a bold step to study the Bible in 2006. I registered for a two-year Evangelical Ministry study in December of 2005. In January 2006, I went to my first class, but when I returned by 10:00 PM, I didn't go back again due to something strange that occurred to me that night.

The incident that occurred that night resulted in the receiving of extra-terrestrial knowledge from a supernatural force. This force put two earphones on me, and only I could hear through them, but my fiancée, children, and everybody around me couldn't hear what I heard.

They were the invisible communication devices a spiritual man put on me so that I alone could hear him and his team of lecturers. They spoke the entire world system to me through those devices, and I took notes wherever I went during those two and a half years (2006-mid 2008).

So, I am what I am today, and I say what I say today, and I don't know how to stop because of the power. I acknowledge God, and I am a witness to what happened then.

He told me to talk about a lot of things, but I can't say all of them.

What are the words "Forces, Energies, and Pressures"?

Human Science is the work of the invisible manifested into the visible. The invisible/unseen forces do all the work that all equipment/devices are designed to do. They're the powers of thrust, power of lift, and power of sound. They're generally categorized as "Forces, Energies, and Pressures."

Imagine that scientists (those who invent material things of this world) do not actually know how the things they create work, but all they do is follow instructions laid down by any invisible force that speaks to them through dreams while asleep or by voice while awake or some may feel heavy impulses [thinking] in their heads all the time about a particular thing and as they think ceaselessly, they may begin to develop something through their imaginative thoughts, which are forces of response to the heart. Sometimes, they see flashes in their eyes that create pictures for them to make a diagram of a particular thing. All the instructions they receive become formulas to write and follow, and each formula becomes a line (a call) for a particular force to come to work.

These invisible forces manifesting science unto mankind are called "Mechanics," pronounced "Mech Anics." Their purpose is to work for the Heavens on earth to produce food for heavenly dwellers. They also need to provide comfort for mankind.

Denotative names

Let's start by learning how our names change all the time.

Let's say a particular man's real name is "John," but when he has a clerical job, he is often addressed as Mr. "Secretary." When he learns how to work with cement to build, he is called "Mason." When he learns woodwork, he is called "Carpenter." When he becomes the head of the nation's leaders, he is called Mr. "President."

While these are all good names/titles without knowledge of evil attachment, there are other names/titles that embody the full knowledge of good and bad, as in the case of doctors, soothsayers/sorcerers and prophets/prophetesses. Other titles are a total embodiment of evil training, as in the case of soldiers and police, which are equivalent to witches/wizards and cultic/occulted churches.

I believe there are people out there set to argue that military and paramilitary are not evil, but the question is: what intent is their training based on that makes them experts in weaponry? And God answers that they're the evil that every government represents. They're the strength that every government depends on in comitting evil in all its forms.

They're trained (nurtured) to take human lives in the name of defense. That's why they are the licensed carriers of arms and ammunition [the permitted killers].

Don't forget, God detests man killing man, so He has given me clarification on His involvement in Israel's wars in Bible days.

Similarly, heavenly creatures' names (titles) vary from one duty they perform to another.

Generally, the words Angels and Demons are their official names known to the religious people to distinguish between the good [angel/messenger] and bad [demon/agent] that are all peoples/spirits of Heavens, but no one knows what their names or titles are when they become creators [makers/builders/manufacturers], or when they become breakers [simplifiers/destroyers] to describe their scientific (creative) capacity.

But let me say right now that all the scientific terms like force, energy, pressure, mineral/vitamin, germ/virus/disease, chemical, and so on are various names (titles) of spirits that manifest themselves on earth to do some good or bad things. So, when human science sees the result of an action that is caused invisibly, they (the same spirits) pour a name on the human's tongue for the thing that had happened.

Always remember, we are nothing without the Spirit. That goes to say we can't do anything without the Spirit.

Why do we have human science?

Their reason for coming to earth to teach mankind how to make things is to speed up their work to provide food for themselves. Even God's reason for creating the earth and human beings is embedded in His need for survival. That secret is hidden in God's commandment for man to keep his/her body holy for Him God. It is further hidden in His commandment for mankind to abstain from promiscuity. The theology there is not suitable, but what I cannot hold on to right now is the fact that mankind has been starving God.

The Bible puts it fine in its own way as mankind is depriving God of his/her body (Temple of God) through the pollution that the body receives from a promiscuous lifestyle.

God preferred marriage (one man to one woman) instead of a random lifestyle to prevent this. However, random lifestyles are now the order of this world system, and marriage has no religious significance other than being a legal matter in the present-day life of mankind. To be clear, let me say that the Heavens need the things (Minerals) of the physical world to survive, and the only way these Heavens receive these things of the earth is through the human body.

So, let's see how the system was designed and could be simplified under the analogy of a human being's ability to make a car or yellow machine to speed up whatever he/she wants to do, whereby he/she goes into the equipment to make it function by touching or pressing down buttons or pushing, and pulling specific parts of the vehicle to enable it to make sound, move, grab, pull, lift, drop, drag, dig and so on.

This is exactly how God made man as His equipment and instrument. He allowed all of His heavenly forces (the spirits of both good and bad) to enter into the human body to operate it for the sole purpose of providing for the Heavens.

So, there is a cycle: Force/Angel acts on a man while man acts on equipment to make things quickly for all.

Now, if you keenly observe this cycle, you will notice that a human being is a complex machine for the spirit, as a car or bulldozer is a complex machine for a human being, all in the name of providing for man, while man provides for the Spirit. That is, man uses equipment to process food faster, and he eats it to survive/live, while the angels and demons also use man to process food for them. This means that all spirits (both angels and demons) feed on the same human body because the human body is a public place for them all. This further means that when we use our man-made equipment to make food, we eat it to obtain energy from the earth's minerals. The spirits, in turn, use us as their equipment to process the food in our bodies' mechanics, and then they come to feed on our bodies to receive the earth's energy, too. How they feed on the human body is done in two separate ways as follows.

The demon spirits primarily derive their food [their food is the 'energy' stored in the foods we eat] from feeding on our flesh and blood [remember your Bible story that says the human body is made of the dust of the ground]. The human body, therefore, contains a wealthy quantity of these minerals, which is why the human body, herein referred to as the flesh and bones, is capable of dissolving back into the ground when life has been taken out. The spirit desires it, which is why human sacrifices are required in different forms in every part of the world.

In ancient times and in some parts of the world today, the idea of offering human blood or parts to shrines explains this theory. In Western countries and growing-technology countries today, wars in all their different forms do explain the same demand for human flesh and blood for the demon world.

Satan uses human blood or flesh to avoid the complications involved in using the primary method, which is the sexual method.

Satan obtains his energy from blood and human parts to minimize [attempting to avoid] the fight over the process of obtaining it from the sexual fluids in the human bowls [sexual areas] where the women's demons concentrate their activities. The angels go there, too.

However, the angels do focus on the primary method of

receiving the energy contained in the earth's minerals from the human body through the food humans eat (check my other title, Interpretation First).

This has been the major secret behind God's demand for virginity before marriage and faithfulness after marriage.

This scenario is why God created physical things such as plants, mammals, fish, and birds to be processed scientifically for good hygiene before eating them. After they have been dissolved into the bloodstream, the forces of the Heavens come into the human body to feed themselves [not right inside the human body, they feed themselves]. They take them to the Heavens in a single batch, where they are further synthesized [separated into different components as needed].

But God is starving nowadays because the angels of God do find it difficult in our modern time to get good food from the body due to bodily pollution through random lifestyles that bring into our bodies different satanic forces that fight against God's angels.

What is the Air around us?

Though we don't see these spirits, we feel them around us in the form of the air that blows on our bodies and the air we breathe, which we feel entering and exiting our bodies. In the EXTRAS section of this book, I have given you a few examples of the practical demonstrations the Spirit had performed on me. However, let's discuss the activities of these spirits from a diagram called "Information Superhighway" that was dictated to me to draw in the analogy of a cross-country highway built in the United States of America called I-80 (Interstate Highway 80).

The "Information Superhighway" that represents Spiritual I-80

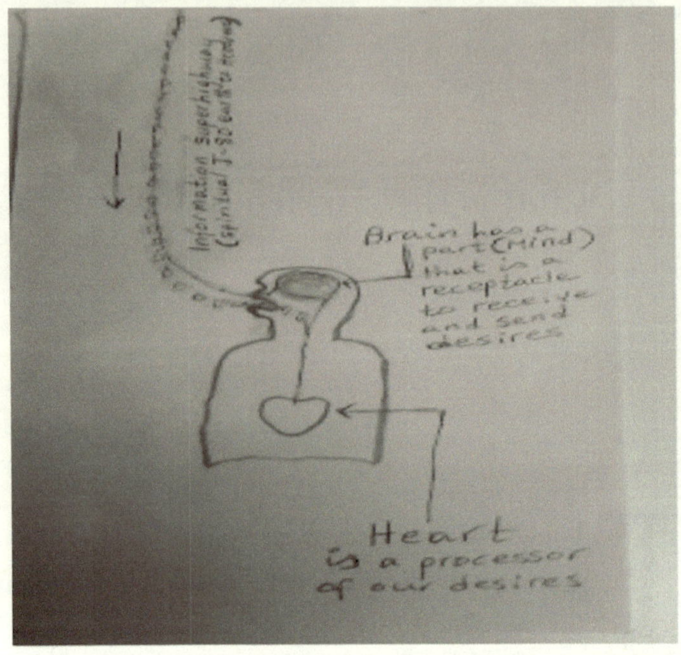

During my practical training from 2006 to 2008, the spirits taught me exactly how the forces work or interact with us.

If I took all my time to explain, I still think that mankind wouldn't believe me, for they wouldn't be able to understand exactly what it is. But I tell you the truth: Our body is the dwelling place of the spirit; it is their house, their village, and we are their instrument and their equipment. They can turn us around in any way they want. Without them, we wouldn't be able to talk, walk, or move any part of our body.

In my intense practical training, the spirits demonstrated this to me. It happened even when I didn't want to open my mouth, but my mouth was forcibly opened while my face looked up to Heaven. I used to feel something jumping into my mouth like an insect would. Before I notice it, it goes straight down my esophagus or oesophagus (colloquially known as the food pipe, food tube, or gullet) and finally into my stomach.

Whenever one of them entered like this, it took a few seconds for me to feel it bubbling into my stomach. Whenever it bubbled up, I felt like it was spreading tentacles through my body just like a Pseudopodium, and eventually, it started to operate on my body without my control. It had the power to lift or put down my hand, to move or stick my foot, to turn or stop turning my head, to make me talk or shut my mouth, to make me sing or laugh, to make me cry or smile and just anything that it desired to make me do to understand how the spirits often operate the human body at its will. The same showed me how sorrow or joy comes to us, and most importantly, I was trained in the way sex fondling works on us.

All of these actions were accompanied by voices in my ears, which explained to me the meaning of anything that flew into my mouth, bubbled up in my stomach, or swollen up in me to take over the body and operate it in the various ways I felt.

At the start, it was very startling and fearful to me, so I screamed, but as days went by, I became used to it and began to appreciate it to understand the things I had previously wondered about. [I was told that this might only happen to someone whom the Spirit has chosen and prepared that person to know so.]

After the training, somewhere in the middle of 2008, a

voice announced that my school with the Spirit was complete, and I was now permitted to go into the world to do as every normal being would. I was told that I would find a job to help me raise money for the books, and through the books, I would have the long-awaited opportunity to travel to the United States, where I would speak to the world about everything.

However, I was not told what kind of job I was supposed to do to get the type of money needed while living as a poor man through the financial support of his maternal sister, who lived in the U.S.

Also, I was not told what I would go through in the U.S.

Fortunately, I got a job and the money to publish my first two books with a UK publishing company called "Authorhouse, U.K." [The books were later canceled and merged with the title *Interpretation First* and this title *Interpretation Second*].

Through the two books, I was invited to a Book Signing event held in Miami, Florida, in 2013. After the event, I went back to Liberia and returned to the U.S. in August 2014 [in an effort] to find ways to get finances for more books and hold speaking events. Thus, I couldn't return due to the Ebola outbreak in Liberia.

However, the road has been rough since I arrived in the USA.

Through it all, the voice said they wouldn't leave me for good; instead, they'd always be with me to guide me through the writing and speaking processes. And when the time comes, the Spirit shall descend on me to give me some demos.

The voice also said it was not going to be easy for me at all, for the road ahead was going to be tough. People were going to doubt me, and many would call me different names.

What makes technology possible?

I was told that nothing works without air because air is the Spirit. This means that the air operates human science (technology) [the air is a mixture of all the forces meeting and passing by one another], so all machines made by scientists have openings to take in air.

The air blows everywhere and makes deposits everywhere, which is why some of these spirits are found in liquids, soil, stone, and plants in the forms of energy, pressure, and force or as viruses and germs in the case of destruction and body breakdown, and as minerals and vitamins in the case of bodybuilding.

When they turn violently against each other, the result somehow feels like a storm, thunder and lightning, or an ocean tide.

The unseen forces (people) have greater power to do things than we can, so they work with us to accomplish what they want to be done. That is why they're found everywhere as deposits in physical things like the woods, the stones, the liquids, the soils, and in anything.

Their presence in physical things makes every aspect of technology use physical things like water, oil, gas/fuel, stone, soil, and wood to come in contact with natural air in order to make science work. This is expressed in a formula as Spirituality + Physicality = Matter [the Equal sign means "Create" something on earth]. What this means is that the forces stored in physical matter must be combined with the forces in heaven (a sphere) to create a reaction that produces things on earth.

Before the science of mineral exploration discovered crude oil and its importance to technology, early science worked with water, wood, stone, and air to make things, and that is how the Steam Engine and the Wood or Coal Engines were developed.

Even now, one such machine that is powered strictly by natural air is the "Injection Molding Machine." One such machine is the "Injection Molding Machine SH 350—Sumitomo," which I worked with in the U.S. on April 25, 2017, to make the white Road Marker that road construction companies use on pavements.

One example is a car that takes gas (stored energy) and burns it with the help of air (driving forces) that enters the combustion chamber.

Imagine how scientists store/keep some power (the battery) to enable us to take it from one place to another, and when you connect it to something else according to their instructions, then you get light, heat, sound, or whatever is required. That's exactly how the air forces are kept in the soil, water, wood, and rocks (physical things to carry around) to be connected/united with other forces of the air (spiritual things man does not see) to produce the desired result.

One thing that scientists know is that when the gas ignites, it explodes into the kind of energy that moves the car. However, they do not understand that some invisible forces contained in the air are distributed to many parts of the vehicle to work together to move or power the vehicle. They act like human beings pushing the vehicle, but they have more power to do so at the fastest speed level.

These forces have more power in thicker fluids than in lighter fluids. That is why they can lift objects a thousand times bigger than they are.

What this means is that they are called "Hydraulics," and when they are compressed in a tube or siphon that compounds them and directs their action to a specific point, they act efficiently and effectively together. Please close your eyes and visualize thousands of people holding hands together to pull something and see how many tons they can remove. But the problem is, why would anyone bring such a massive number of people together to do such work as a bull-dozer, a crane, or a trailer does?

These forces (men and women of the unseen world) who come to work on earth have created a system of convergence and divergence to unite efforts and share powers to comfort the world. This is what the Electric Generator is about.

In an electric-producing machine, the anode (converging point) and the cathode (diverging point) of forces acting together [at this time, the name of these forces change, and science may call them "electrons"], but are actually called 'electons/elect-ions.'

"Ions" are the tiniest [children], simplest of the forces acting together.

The forces (electrons) send out the little ones (ions). Still, these little ones are Spiritually powerful so that they can penetrate faster through mediums to quickly unite with other little ones that are called "chemicals" to form some reaction that may produce light, heat, sound, cold, breeze, and or lift, slide, roll and so forth as we see electrical appliances and equipment do each day in our lives.

Do you think I'm talking nonsense here? No, I'm not, but you're right because you don't understand how all this works.

But see if you can agree with me from this scenario: You own and use a cell phone every day, but you don't have the slightest idea of how it works to do everything it does for you. Do you really have to care about how the magic works? No, all you have to be concerned about is how to use it for the reasons you got it. This is just how Spirituality works and is why it is foolishness to mankind. This is why it is useless to explain what doesn't seem fit, but it fits.

The giant machine

Do you know that every electric generating machine has been modeled to suck in air? Now, I tell you that the air entering the machine is actually the forces of heaven that are getting to work. So, they may first converge/meet somewhere before diverging/dividing/distributing to many other parts of the same machine to do different kinds of work as they come into contact with other properties (chemicals) to react with.

This means that a single generator's electrons (electric current) are responsible for doing so many different works for mankind when they come in contact with other properties at different destinations. This means when electrons (electric current) are produced in a generator, and they flow into a device like a fridge (a refrigerator) where other properties are kept waiting for them to meet to react together, a different matter is produced as dew to make things cold or to turn liquid into solid. But when these same electrons go on to other devices (electric iron, stove, heater ...) to meet other properties, they help to produce heat even as they continue to enter other electrical appliances in a building to do other works.

This scenario of one giant machine (Generator) sitting in one place and doing so many other things in different locations is what explains how God (the one Creator) sits in one place (in Heaven) to do so many things in Heaven and on earth. He is that Giant Machine in Heaven that works with many heavenly dwellers to produce heat (Sun), cold, and rain in heaven while producing wood, soil, and stone on earth.

Enablement of communication

A man-made communication system is the work of the forces of the air. They came down in dispensations (generations by generations) to replace traditional travel done on foot to carry messages or to describe people's looks.

These forces are the ones that fly in the air with our voices and images from one point to another by responding to our heart desires. They may collect a person's voice or photo and present it to another person (s) in a different location just at the measure of the person who makes a call or sends the image.

This explains the wave systems that human science calls the "Sound Wave, Radio Wave, and Electromagnetic Wave."

The Western world has more jobs because

In Heaven (Jerusalem Above), no one is required to buy and sell, so technology has no place to provide jobs for people to earn their living.

However, in Aquebus (Satan's Enclave), where the ownership system and discrimination originated, technology has been brought to earth as a source of livelihood [the means of living].

Now that we know that the science of this world is dispensed among the three races (three human colors) by seniority level, the news I bring is to tell the world why white people [they called themselves "Western people"] are leading in technology and thus have a surplus of jobs in their countries. [seniority is about which color was made first in Heaven before the other, as demonstrated by the fractional distillation method in human science].

So, because the black color was the third [last] of three

major colors to have come out of that Spiritual manufacturing system, black people fell to the last list to develop technology to provide them jobs in their places.

That is why Africa and every corner of the world need technology to create the wealth and jobs needed to stabilize the movement of people from one country to another or, better still, reduce (if not eradicate) one nation's dependency on another.

Imagine if the entire world were covered with technology and its riches. Automatically, the world would develop, and everywhere would become suitable for mankind to enjoy God's natural gifts. The book *Interpretation Third* teaches more of this.

And when the entire world becomes technologically developed and industrialized, it automatically becomes united and comfortable, and its people become friends but not foes. There will be no rich and no poor people, there will be no suffering and no needy people, there will be no room for envy and jealousy, and there will be neither killers nor robbers, there will be no fight over tech control between superpowers like is currently happening in the time of this book.

That's why the world's most prosperous and technologically advanced countries must unite to develop the underdeveloped countries. Technology sharing is essential and godly. Adopting new economic means to continue providing comfortable lives for everyone should be the most critical priority for nations now.

I mean, a united world with infrastructural developments throughout describes the following system (next world) to come after this system that Satan damaged with greed, pride, jealousy, envy, selfishness, wars, sensuality, sexuality, and subversion of God's word.

Part Three

About black race and government systems

The Underdevelopment Issues in Africa

[Egypt is considered the ancient place of science, but where is Egypt ranked among the best technology countries?]

Egyptians are a mix of two primary human colors: those who look like Middle Eastern people (semi-white people from Asia) and those who look like Sub-Saharan Africans (early residents of Africa).

That's why Egyptian history has been examined under a different race, so Africa, as a black race, should not take pride in Egyptian history.

Also, I'm inserting Egyptian history here to set the stage for racial hierarchy.

This means Africans (both semi-whites and blacks) are proud to loudly say that civilization began in Africa, which they use to refer to how scientific knowledge (advanced methods of agriculture, construction, and medicine) had a more significant bearing on the practices of ancient Egypt.

Biblical history confirms the uniqueness of the Egyptians. It tells us the early lives of Israelis [originally called Hebrews] who worked as slaves in Egypt to help build Egyptian cities in ancient times.

But in that story, I've been told that God's secret agenda was also to use the time for them to learn from those Egyptians so that if they went to their promised land, they would have used the knowledge from Egypt to build their own land.

Reading this kind of history and seeing the industrial level of Israel compared to Egypt today brings me sadness because this tells us that the Egyptians were more knowledgeable than the Hebrews/Jews [originally the Ur people] at that time, coupled with the number of dispensations these two peoples passed through is sufficient indication that Egyptians should be the ones leading in knowledge in terms of human science from that time to present.

In fact, Egypt must be the country leading in scientific knowledge by now and must be able to provide the kind of job opportunities technologically advanced countries are providing today in the Western world.

By now, Egypt must be the country to which other Africans risk going for greener pastures, but not Israel.

So, the question is: Why is reality the opposite of Egypt and the rest of Africa?

While drafting the first manuscript of this book in 2018, I searched the internet to rank Egypt among the best technology countries in the world. I didn't see anything specific, but don't worry; I can answer why Egypt is far below the ranks.

Still, I didn't limit this to Egypt alone; instead, I

expanded my thoughts to the entire African continent, which has always remained a beggar to the white world.

As I was one of every refugee scrambling during the Liberian civil war for resettlement to the white man's countries, two more questions popped up: [1]Why do we flood European countries and America? And [2]Why do they have so much advantage over us?

I have answers to these questions, which you will learn later.

Is there a science of invention in black Africa?

So, while I asked these questions in my mind, I still couldn't forget the stories my grandfather told me most times when he was in his right mind to lecture me, most especially when I reached the age of 10, that's when he used to take me to the farm each year to help him with the farm work; brush, fell trees and clean.

He told me that everything they used before the Europeans (the explorers) came to Africa was made by skillful and gifted people among them (the black people). He said things like clothes, pots & pans, cutlasses [Americans say machetes] & axes, guns, salt & pepper, and others were made (manufactured) by themselves, the black people.

In fact, he gave me two African-made implements, a cutlass & an axe, which I used the first time to work before he bought any European or American-made farming tools for me.

Hearing these stories about the early stages of human

science in Africa, I was startled that they had science but neglected to improve every aspect of their sciences. Rather, they (Africans) ended up chasing after European products like clothes, tobacco, salt, firearms, and so on, for which the sale of their tribal war captives became a lucrative trade that supplied African slaves to the European markets and thus fueled more wars and divisions among themselves on the continent.

This is to say that my tribesmen had lost or abandoned their sciences by the time I was born. Instead, they had gone under dark science, which has long been branded as "witch practices." They refused to improve on many positive things among the signs/sciences that they used in the so-called witch world, but rather, they kept [still keep] them reclusive. For example, they could build airplanes and fly in them to go wherever they want to, and they could build skyscrapers that they live in in the Dark World. They even do what I now know in technology countries to be "Cyberwar – spying and attacking another behind closed doors."

To this, I have two stories. For the first, while I was in my teens in my hometown, Putuken, my grandfather, Oldman Ben Doe Jah, was one of what they used to refer to as the "powerful men of the town" who used to meet in secret gatherings to deliberate on crucial matters, like when the people begin to experience a strange sickness in the town. He was 80 by the time I was 12 in the year 1980. At age 12, I was initiated into the secret society of men in my hometown, which qualified me to hear deep secrets of the land.

My tribe is called Grebo in Southeastern Liberia. The Grebo people don't have a society for women, but

they have one for men. It is called the Qwee Society. Every child between the ages of 12 and 14 is required to join it. The society is primarily intended to train boys into manhood. The training incorporates working and wrestling skills. However, other things are fetish about it.

So, every Grebo boy child can only be considered a man after joining their society. Why? Because he is exposed to the activities of their gods.

That's why my grandfather would now tell me the secret things of their land.

This was when he would tell me how he was chosen during tribal wartime to bear a certain charm on his back as a point man. That charm would cry aloud on his back like a young baby to alert them whenever they were approaching an ambush. He further told me how he was given some other powers that would neutralize bullets whenever an enemy shot at him unaware, and no bullet would penetrate his body.

In our town, my grandpa showed me one woman, Ma Sarah, who was often accused of witchcraft. Still, whenever the youths of the town protested against the atrocities of this woman and demanded that she be put to death, the older men [often my grandpa's group] would reject the killing of the woman. [The older men are the councilmen who must sanction anything before it can be done.]

I asked my grandpa one day why they wouldn't let this woman die when other men and women who had committed the same crimes had been killed.

The Grebo people use a specific tree they call "Sassy

wood," which they believe has some power to know who is guilty of a crime or not guilty. So, they would have the accused peel out the hardback of the tree, beat it in a mortar, pour water on it, and sift the water before drinking it after chanting out whether he/she is guilty or not guilty.

So, whoever is guilty of whatever crime and drank the sassy wood would die after a few minutes or an hour, but not guilty would vomit it out to be free of it.

This is how many people considered the witches and wizards were killed through the sassy wood, Ma Sarah couldn't be permitted by the elders to go close to it. Let's continue to see why.

Grandpa laughed over my question before telling me the secret reason.

He said the woman was "a woman in man's clothing," doing more than most men would do in the Dark World. He said whenever there was any crucial case like a strange illness or anything foreign to what they knew, the influential folks [those of magical powers] usually gathered in the bush to deliberate or cast lots. He said during this session the only woman who would attend such a gathering of men was the Sarah woman. [I mean, there is a secret spot prepared in the bush near the town where men of the secret society meet on special occasions to get away from the listening ears of women and other men [foreign men] who are not members of the society].

No one, particularly women, can spy on them whenever they're in a meeting. Whenever anyone is caught doing so, there is a severe punishment, including death after repeated action.

So, Grandpa said she was not only a powerful witch among the witches and wizards but also an undercover woman the men would send to any town they found responsible for their problems.

Grandpa said that on such a journey, she would fly at night or day and pose as a visitor who lodges with any friend or relative in the town. She would perform all the signs and wonders required to counterattack the enemy town and its witches. After staying a few or many days doing what she went to do, she would return home safely.

Grandpa said in the witch world, this type of work that comes from a bloodthirsty spirit required a human sacrifice, which was why the woman would kill anyone as part of her sacrifice after her mission.

He said this was where the woman would remind the town folks and make them guilty of any decision to put her to death because of any killing she might have done.

When this story was told, I might not have understood why a human being would be used for a sacrifice to appease the power that protects the people.

Still, as I was writing my manuscript in 2018, I could see a similarity in modern military operations. I have seen in war videos where a group of soldiers would send a person or a few to die during fierce combat with the sole purpose of saving a large population of people. Technologically advanced countries' warplanes would choose to blow up infrastructures with a minimum civilian population only if it meant a way to save an entire city from falling to mass killing by enemies.

For the second story, during my practical training in 2008, I obtained spiritual eyes and ears that enabled me to see things and hear voices in the spirit. This was done to teach me the lessons on spiritual preachers and healers-how they get the powers they use, and how they see the things they see and talk about.

On one occasion, I was quickened to my feet without knowing why. So, I went to visit a paternal brother of mine. When I got there, I met him and his family about to eat. The spirit didn't allow me to enter. I stopped at the door. After a few minutes, my brother's stepdaughter began to cry, holding down her stomach and screaming, "My stomach is hurting. It's hurting hard." She said, "Mum, I want to vomit; please take me outside," and she screamed harder.

They took her out toward the grass away from the house, but she didn't vomit; rather, she just spat a little spit (saliva) on the ground while the pain persisted. "My husband, we need to take her to the hospital very quickly," the mother said to my brother. Then the Spirit came down on me right away in the usual manner by jumping into my mouth like an insect, and a voice came out of me saying, "Bring her here to me," and they brought her right by me. Then I said {it was the Spirit speaking through me though}, "Stop, she is under attack." They stopped, and I raised my right hand in the air, and I spoke in a certain language like the church prophets would say "tongue," and when I stretched out my hand to the little girl's mouth for a few seconds, I told them she was healed.

The mother insisted that they take her to the hospital,

but my brother said they should wait for a while. After a few minutes, the little girl said she was okay.

Then the Spirit came down on me again, and a voice came out of my mouth saying, "You guys should ask your bigger daughter; she'll tell you what happened." She wasted no time explaining the whole story when they turned to her. She said they, the three children, were eating together, but the boy, my brother's nephew, spat in the food, and the spit became the poison that the little girl took in. She said the spit poison was intended to initiate the little one into their witch world.

During this revelation, she told her parents that the boy was a King in the Kingdom of Darkness, rich with houses blazing with gold and electric current. She said this boy had initiated her against her will and was attempting to initiate the little sister while she, the bigger sister, had been protesting against all the acts. She said she could not stop or subdue him as he was a King in that world.

In the two scenarios above, the mighty woman in a man's clothing lived impoverished. She tramps on her feet in the day like all other people do. She rides in cars whenever she goes along with others where the car road goes, but she rides in the plane of the Dark world whenever she's alone.

The boy, a King in the Dark world, lives with his uncle, who struggles daily to find food for them. He lives in his uncle's zinc roundhouse, where they have no electricity, but his wealth in the Dark world is beyond measure. What a people!!!

Since Satan is the ruler of this age who is also behind the science of technology in technology countries where he

(Satan) creates both good sciences (the comfort we get from the use of air conditional, vehicles, airplanes, life-saving drugs, the body wears, electricity and so on) and bad sciences (the pollution of the air with carbon emission, life taking drugs, disease making chemicals, heavy arm artilleries, B-bomber warplanes, chemical weapons, nuclear weapons, hydrogen and atomic bombs and all that threatens the peaceful existence of mankind); witches in Africa also possess the very ability to do good (powers of healing, protecting and creating) while doing evil (powers of destruction through killing and, powers of inflicting pains and hardships through sickness and hold downs.)

Because of their hidden arts, Africans have not been able to advance above the medieval lifestyle and are unable to handle their own crises.

If they should be labeled as people of science, they must vigorously and proudly transform their traditional practices into technology science and let the world see what they have to contribute to the modern science of invention. But until then, they have no science of invention. What they have remains dark because it doesn't benefit the majority.

Why do black people look up to the white people?

I remember back in the 80s, when I was yet in Junior High School, when we used to do current events, and most news dominating the African stories were about war and drought: war about Eritrean Rebels and drought in Ethiopia, Sudan, and Mozambique. These African countries were suffering from natural and man-made disasters. Still, their help came from the white people who organized their resources under the brand "United Nations," which air-dropped humanitarian supplies to cater to malnourished African children and their starving families.

Yet, 16 years later, I found myself in the same situation: the United Nations had to deliver humanitarian supplies to Liberian Refugees outside the country and to those displaced inside the country.

In terms of ending the war in Liberia, Liberians had to look up to the United States of America and the UN to come to end their civil crises and the one in Sierra Leone. Then again, I asked, why must the white man have to do everything for the black man before it gets better?

When I think of all this, I say, what the heck is wrong with Africa? But in all this, I didn't know that the answer to black backwardness was just right in the corner to come to me as the Spirit world was there watching over me in my restless situation of pondering every day over the lack of advancement on the Continent of Africa.

Why do white people seem superior?

Before I got the correct answer to whether the white man is superior or not, I can still remember 1999 when I first grasped the idea of the homogeneity (sameness) of three countries in the world, two of which are white settlements and one of which is a black settlement. I couldn't believe that the two white settlements were among the most developed countries in the world while the black country was far down in comparison.

In analyzing the white man's and black man's thinking, I found that everywhere the white man went, he improved the place he occupied, but wherever the black man went, his place was not comparably improved. The three homogeneous countries on the planet were established by settlers from foreign lands.

The three countries founded by Settlers (Strangers) are South Africa, North America, and Liberia.

South Africa

Figure 1: View of Johannesburg, South Africa. The work of white migrants in Africa.

In the year 1488, a European (Portuguese) named Bartholomeu Diaz discovered South Africa while finding an alternative route to the Indies as there was a great struggle between the Muslim world and the Christendom that made land passage to the Indies difficult for Europeans in search of spices such like cinnamon, ginger, pepper, and so on.

Bartholomeu's discovery of South Africa opened trade between South African hunters and Europe.

Also, in 1867, a 15-year-old boy named Erasmus Jacobs discovered a 21.25-carat diamond known as the Eureka diamond, which opened a gush of Europeans to this place, and this new entry was nicknamed the "Diamond Rush" into South Africa.

The Whites (British) who took over the place have been the ones who turned it into a developed country today.

There is no argument that the picture you see above is the brain work of the white man, and that is why South Africa today looks like a European country.

United States of America

In 1492, another European named Christopher Columbus from Italy inadvertently discovered a land across the Atlantic as he chose to sail west until he reached the Indies. This became another trade ground where the Europeans flourished. The new land became more favorable to the Europeans, who subsequently battled and conquered the indigenous Indians.

Figure 2: View of Washington DC, United States of America

Figure 2: View of Washington DC, United States of America https://pixabay.com/photos/washington-monument-washington-dc-c-1627184/

Today, the land that was taken from the Indians has become the world's most powerful economy, a well-developed country with the world's strongest military, and a leader in everything.

The ideas that shaped the history of the land came from white migrants/visitors/invaders, sometimes called "friends from Europe" and beyond.

Liberia

Figure 3: View of Monrovia, Liberia, West Africa (Shutterstock Image ID: 1225877989)

In Africa, a similar migration and occupation system occurred in a small place now called Liberia, in the South of West Africa.

It happened when a group of black people were shipped, if not to say "dumped," into Africa in the 18th century after so many years of stay in the United States of America, where they labored hard as slaves [powerful human machines] in the building of the new land from colony to country.

Abolitionists founded Liberia

Some people say the growth of Christianity led to the rejection of slavery. Still, I take exception to that based on the fact that Christianity existed in England and didn't put a stop to the practice of slavery in England and now in Newfoundland. Therefore, I attribute the abolition of slavery to science, which brought about the invention of equipment to replace the slow process of human efforts.

This is to emphasize that the advent of the Industrial Revolution in the 18th century [even though it is a term used to describe Britain's economic development from 1760–1840] marked the beginning of the lesser need for human efforts in some work areas. For example, for easy and fast transportation of goods, the train was invented in 1804 by Richard Trevithick in Wales, England. The first tractor for agriculture work was built in 1892 by John Froelich in Clayton County, Iowa, USA.

What I see is that Christianity only played a vital role in

the area of finding an alternative place to get the free people out when they outlived their usefulness and became condemned to live among the whites.

Due to those ugly things the white people said about the few free blacks, moved a man named Robert Finley, who founded an organization in 1816 that was branded "The American Colonization Society" (ACS) to champion the movement behind setting blacks free and relocating the free people from America.

So, what did those people say about the free blacks? They said the free blacks would be unable to assimilate into the white society of the United States of America. In fact, John Randolph, one famous slave owner, called free blacks "promoters of mischief." This is why on December 21, 1816, a group of exclusively white upper-class males, including James Monroe, after whom the capital city of Liberia was named, Bushrod Washington, I believe after whom a little piece of Island in Monrovia was named, and a few others held a meeting in Washington D.C., and one week later adopted a constitution.

They worked hard for three years and finally sent 88 black emigrants to West Africa with three white ACS agents and thus established a black colony in that part of Africa now called "Liberia."

The ACS employed white agents to govern the settlement, but the colony rejected the idea of white control over the blacks again. So, in 1842, Joseph Jenkins Roberts became the first non-white governor of the colony. In 1847, the colony declared itself an independent state, with its black governor, J.J. Roberts, elected as its first president.

Why I say blacks lack innovation

In Liberia, people argued that America didn't develop the country, unlike what the French and British did for their colonies before granting them independence. Still, I disagree, arguing that the American people would have done so if they had been allowed to rule the blacks for a longer period of time.

Imagine that in Liberian history books written before their civil war, it is recorded that the U.S. government refused to recognize Liberia's independence because they argued that the Colony was not mature enough to have governed itself independently, a period of non-recognition that ran from July 26, 1847, to February 5, 1862.

Judging from the Americans' argument, I believe that the white man, this time the American man, may have had the willingness in mind to develop this African nation born of a black colony before granting them independence later.

Despite the resistance against a second white rule and the

insistence on early independence from the white man, these blacks in this country of migrants failed to develop the place where they settled and called their home, unlike what the white migrants did both in South Africa and in North America (now the United States.) They failed to develop the country despite the freedom they found in this place with the abundance of gold, diamond, timber, iron ore, and the enormous sales made to the world market in its 142 years of independence before going into civil war in December 1989. They failed to develop the country even when the country became the world's largest rubber-producing nation at one time in the country's history.

The failure of these black migrants in Liberia to do just as the white migrants did for their countries has given me reasons to question the black's ability to innovate/revolutionize.

Black Africa, as with other continents

Continentally, Black Africa, with all of its natural riches and long history of trade relations with the White World, has not been able to develop advanced manufacturing techniques (technology). They neglected every bit of science that they knew, even before the white man came to them.

Figure 4: View of New Delhi, India ***Royalty-free stock photo ID: 563982820***

A lot of people argue that Africa's underdevelopment is due to colonization and corruption, but I differ here again because I see colonization as something that took place in other countries around the world, and those countries have now emerged as not only developed ones but also world powers.

For example, **Colonialism** took place in India by the

Dutch, French, Portuguese, and the British. Also, some parts of China were colonized by almost all-powerful Western countries and Japan. But today, India is no longer a developing [poor and un-industrialized] country but a rising industrial power. At the same time, China is not just a strong economic and industrial power in Asia but also participating in space exploration with the U.S., Russia, and Japan.

Currently, China is on equal footing with the most advanced industrial country, the USA, in terms of technology and development. Also, China and India are now leading the new bloc, BRICS, of developmental interest to help revolutionize how underdeveloped countries can be developed.

So, if these countries are now among the industrial nations in the world today, then show me one black African country that is not governed by whites that is industrialized.

The fact that African countries are no longer under white occupations is clear proof that they have the power to make economic decisions about how to wisely use the money they receive from bilateral and multilateral trades combined with multimillion loans and grants they receive from friendly countries and financial institutions around the world. Still, a major factor is the lack of willingness to do the right thing and stop relying on others for everything.

One other thing that seems so blurry to me is that [maybe] black people lack self-confidence in themselves; they take so much pride in other people's things more than they should love their own things, and in that way, they may start to improve their own handwork.

What I'm talking about is that black people have long

ago accepted that everything they do is evil, and that has [probably] discouraged black science so that when the white man was improving from using traditional methods [herbal ways] of treatments, the black man said his own was evil, so he sat complacently.

The inheritability of corruption

A study on the topic of corruption in Africa revealed that African countries inherited this attitude of corrupt governance from the white man during colonialism. The study revealed that in most African colonies, these political, economic, and civil powers were centralized by colonial powers, who reserved all the top jobs and education for their fellow colonists.

Sadly, in the colony, the judiciary, law, police, and security services, which are institutions that should serve as watchdogs for society against corruption, served only the elites by obeying the colonial administrator.

The private sector, primarily producing materials for export to the originating country of imperial power like France, Great Britain, Portugal, and Italy, seldom held the colonial government accountable because it depended on the mother country for subsidies, licenses, and contracts.

In the colonial world, the media was also controlled with few exceptions.

Then came the period of independence [This I called 'quasi-independence' since African countries are still dictated to by European nations that colonized them. This is what became vivid to me in 2003 when the indigenous Ivoirians started a civil war. A discussion popped up on the issue of Western intervention, whereby it became incumbent upon France to intervene because she was called the mother country of that West African nation since she (France) colonized that country. Of course, the Paris government quickly moved in with air bombers and infantry soldiers, which quelled the situation and paved the way for peace talks between the opposing factions

in the conflict. France's action followed the US's involvement in Liberia's civil conflict].

Incidentally, this may change in a few years to come if the current trend of resistance and advocacy initiated by a few French-speaking African countries like Burkina Faso, Niger, and Mali continues as of the time of this publication. These countries are resisting quasi-independence, seeking total independence from France to make decisions for themselves and control their economic system by negotiating foreign investments and choosing their friends independently. They oppose foreign rule.

The African colonial leaders were replaced by the Independent Movement Aristocracy, who became the dominant independent leader and his "struggle families," often the ethnic group of the leader or political party. This means

African movements are highly dominated by one leader, his ethnic or regional group, or his political base.

Being an African, I conceded with the fact that the indigenous people of most African countries were "relatively" poor, unskilled, and without significant holdings in the private sector at the on-set of independence uprising [I was wondering why the writer (s) used the word 'most' rather than 'all' African countries because even the few that had acquired education didn't have enough money].

The report says that very few people from the grassroots had professional careers outside the struggle, so they had to be given jobs after the struggle, which became very fertile ground for corruption.

Now, the practice of merit-based appointments was out of importance, along with this system of giving jobs to members of the same family or ethnic group and political party. This gruesome practice of no merit-based thing for unqualified friends and families appointed to manage key public institutions has resulted in no or low impacts on reforms in Africa.

Partly for these reasons, the after-mark effect is that post-independence Africans' private sectors are quiet and are not able to demand accountability from governments.

In some instances, the liberation movement government embarks on a policy of creating a "capitalist class" or new "Indigenous" businesspeople, sometimes called "Black Economic Empowerment (BEE) or Indigenization Programs."

But this is the shielded way political leaders get holdings in newly privatized public companies, get state tenders to supply some services for the government, or get a few private companies owned by foreign or former colonial companies.

Beneficiaries of these programs don't hold African governments accountable at the end of the equation. [Um, when I got to this portion of the discussion, I took a deep breath, reflecting on the inaction of foreign governments in whose territories corrupt African leaders flee or take their corrupt sums of money for keep despite whatever accusations come out of Africa.]

And then there is this shining lifestyle [big cars, big houses, large parties, womanizing (so many girlfriends and so much money on their caretaking), and so many foreign trips] that African government leaders live even while their citizens cry daily for economic hardships.

I have wondered about the origin of such behavior in my home country, but it was not until 2018 that I decided to search Google for evidence of corruption reports in Africa for this book. Then, I learned that the root of wastefulness started with the small colonial leaders who lived shining lifestyles during their rule in Africa. And when the writer (s) say a culture of hard work was lacking in these people, I agree fully because they spent very little time doing the people's work than they spent on making appointments with girlfriends, meeting them at various times and locations and having parties in the day or night.

It's unfortunate that many post-independence African leaders modeled their lifestyles on those of the colonial leaders as a way of demonstrating their success.

That's why it shouldn't surprise anyone who finds any poor African with a flashy lifestyle, which is the same reason he/she may not see anything wrong with the flamboyant ways of his/her leaders.

Agreed, Europeans or white people are also corrupt, but the difference I see is what they do at home with their wealth and what the African people (black people) do at home with their portion of wealth. This is what pushed me to identify three kinds of human corruption and their effects:

1. **White corruption** is the one that does not hate the society it preys on, but it develops American and European societies. It strives very hard to build the nation, develops the economy, and supports innovation (check how White Millionaires & Billionaires support projects) that makes white people leaders of the things we do as people so that even the poor receive clean drinking water, electricity, and the basic things every man needs.

I'm talking about the support method of innovations (development of new ideas) that has enabled white people to know no border of weather so that even in hot seasons, they grow food so much that they have a surplus to offer/sell to others.

The highest innovation attained in science in the West has grown to what is now known as technology. This has enabled the West to provide food to Africans during natural and self-made crises like drought, famine, and wars. The West's support for innovations in technology has provided them with millions of jobs in their lands and has created beauty in their cities. Now, for these jobs and the beauty of their cities, Africans are flooding their lands.

2. **Semi-white corruption** exists with skin color that lies between white and black or has not been recognized by European men as white. This is about how other people outside the Eurozone innovate too [Middle Eastern people, far Eastern Asians like the Chinese and their types, and Asiatic Indians and their types].

These people differ from blacks because they have a similar thinking faculty to white people (European people, including Americans).

They're also humans with corrupt minds, but they strive harder to compete with the white man.

I see them as jealous of the white man but constructive in their jealousy. This can be seen from the story of the Meiji regime (Meiji Restoration of 1868-1912) in Japan, which chose to catch up with the Europeans and the Americans. By so doing, they sent students to the Western world to learn Western Railroads, factories, and communications systems, which eventually led to a great sale of manufactured goods to foreign countries for Japan, thus making Japan a strong economic power in East Asia today.

Another demonstration of the semi-white people's good thinking is found when some Asian and North African countries sell their natural resources (particularly oil) to the white man and use the money to buy technology to manufacture goods and even make weapons of mass destruction in their countries just as the white man does at home.

This color of humankind builds their cities as well as does the white man, and they're in technological competition with the white man day by day, unlike the black man.

Figure 4: View of Tehran, Iran (Asia) https://pixabay.com/photos/tehran-iran-persia-landscape-642743/ Figure 5: View of Algiers, Algeria (North Africa) ***Royalty-free stock photo ID: 1103677298***

Black corruption is that human form of corruption that hates its own society. It has the practice of ignoring self-development and innovation but priding in others.

Studying colonial activities made me realize that the system was a two-way benefit. The Europeans saw certain things, whether human resources or other resources, in each African area that they were interested in, and that triggered them to use both force and persuasion to get them. On the other hand, each African kingdom had its interest, whether by selling their captured slaves or other resources to the "invaders" or Europeans; the same triggered them to either surrender or freely accept the strangers.

However, while the Europeans took away the resources from Africa to build their home countries, which we see shining today, the Africans totally neglected to build their own countries with what they got from the bargain.

In the worst-case scenario, the Africans took their wealth to the white man's country for keep, and both the wealth of the white business partners and the black partners were used [are still used] by the white man to build white nations. Yet the African man went begging and still goes begging to the white man for aid.

Please search the internet for 'Africa's wealth floods offshore as corrupt leaders'

Let's see what a media report on October 20, 2012, contained about a report from "Global Financial Integrity, a Washington-based nonprofit that traces illicit money" while discussing the topic "Africa's wealth floods offshore as corrupt leaders, corporations use banks to hide fortunes:

Please search the internet for *'Africa's wealth floods offshore as corrupt leaders'*

The Global Financial Integrity report says, "An estimated $1 trillion gets stolen from developing countries in a typical year. "The Organization for Economic Cooperation and Development, a Paris-based nongovernmental group that tracks global economics, compares this with the $134 billion a year in aid that developing countries receive.

The Economic Cooperation and Development report states that the difference saddles these countries with crumbling infrastructure, inadequate food supplies, and scant health care.

While criticisms by some African leaders have been offered in the general investigative report given under the caption, "Africa's elites are plundering their countries," in the Panama Paper on October 18, 2017, from a group of African journalists concerning the growing impact of corruption on

Africa, I do give applause to that which took a detailed look at four African countries and their leaders namely: Togo, Mozambique, Democratic Republic of Congo (DRC) and Botswana.

Togo -The report focused on Togo for its [alleged] mismanagement of funds received from sales of the country's vast reserves of phosphate, which were directly managed [arguably] from the offices of President Faure Gnassinge, whose family has ruled the West African country for 50 years.

The report reveals that Togo earns 40 percent of its export earnings from the mineral, which is crucial for making fertilizers.

In my view, the report sought to find out how much wealth percentage phosphate would generate for the country's development if it weren't being sold for two-thirds of the going rate to a "shady" shipping family called "Gupta."

The report found a similar situation in **Mozambique**, where half of the world's rubies are mined but where the Panama Paper reported dozens of generals, ministers, and high-ranking party members holding ruby licenses.

In this case, I was shocked by the report that the country's ruling elites have forcibly removed villagers from their traditional lands. And despite millions in ruby royalties to the government, the paper says there is no record of this money ever arriving back in these impoverished communities.

Then, in **Botswana**, Panama's report says tourism is the preferred method of plundering the country's coffers. So it seems that tourism here is not only attractive to the likes of the UK's Prince Harry and US talk show queen Oprah

Winfrey but very lucrative, so much so that the President of that country, Ian Khama, along with his relatives and friends, virtually controls the industry through interests in major agencies, channeling profits offshore.

When I saw the word "**Tax**," I immediately concluded that DR Congo had adopted a US's complex tax scheme for development purposes. Still, NO, it's a foreign word for the country's presidential family. This came out of whether the Kabila family pays taxes at all. At the same time, it remains an open secret that the family controls almost all sectors of the economy through a veritable empire of more than eighty companies inside and outside the country, from telecommunications to mining.

The report quotes Jason Stearns, Director of the US-based Congo Research Group, who says it is difficult to estimate the assets of the Congolese presidential family because their commercial network is "completely opaque."

So Sterns says no one knows the value of the different family companies or where they are located or registered.

While all of this tells how rich Africa is despite the lack of technological know-how for processing what it has as its natural gifts, these revelations, no matter how half-truth they are, reveal the true nature of the black race.

It's the same reason that I strongly wish Liberia was not left out: It has been the oldest independent nation in Africa and yet the worst example of how black corruption has held Africa down.

I want to say further that the focus on Liberia is to pinhole every eye to this tiny nation located at the seacoast of

West Africa where black migrants (free slaves) from America live.

They said they had received enlightenment in America, thus inferred by the word "benighted," which happened to appear in the nation's history books by one of their writers, A. Dorris Banks, to describe the people of the various tribes they met on their new land. It is this group of black people who turned the practice of governing into a sole proprietorship wherein [I think] about 99% of the governing body became a single group (freed slaves called "Americo Liberians") who distributed the nation's wealth overnight for themselves without carrying on infrastructural developments for the benefit of the masses. They didn't show the light (civilization/refinement) they claimed to have seen in America.

This practice of self-interest above national development, I repeat, above national development, unlike the ways of the Americans, has obstructed the nurturing of sincerity in every sector of work in the country.

The practice of using government jobs to develop oneself without the slightest thought of preparing the nation's human resources in general to handle the future ably has become a norm even among modern indigenes.

Everybody knows how bad corruption [craving, diverting, and doing the wrong things] is on the country's development, but the nation has yet to see a new generation of people stand up to combat it. A visit to Africa's oldest republic (171 years by 2018) will expose how backward that country is to the visitor, and that is to explain what blacks can do alone in the case of Liberia.

Therefore, I see no proof of *colonialism* and *corruption* as factors responsible for

Africa's continuous under-development, but I rather tell everyone the secrets behind the racial or natural retardation of the Black Race. I mean, giving this secret is telling why the black race has not been able to acquire the ability to excel in all things like the other two races.

The homogeneity of the two white settlements and the one black settlement extends to the kind of self-esteem it bestowed on them, the migrants, who later subdued the indigenes and thus established one central government system over them and have risen to power and wealth over the indigenes of the places they occupied.

Why did the black man seek freedom?

From ancient history, when God allowed the Israelis to go into slavery in Egypt, the spirit told me was to afford them the opportunity to learn from the Egyptians so that they would have gained the skills to use to build a nation after going to their promised land full of milk and honey.

The possession of technological knowledge [Israel got more advanced by its close ties and learning from the Americans] is evidence that today's Israel surpassed Egypt because of its special relationship with the white race (Americans), making the country one of the most beautiful places on earth where Africans seek opportunities.

Like the Jews who the Egyptians enslaved, the Europeans and North Americans also enslaved black Africans. However, the attitude of these free black slaves, now in Liberia, still doesn't explain what they learned during their stay in slavery or why they even sought to be independent of the American [white] people.

Personally, the most shocking thing and [perhaps] the best reason why I pondered over black's conduct for several years is that instead of these free slaves focusing on building Liberia's infrastructures (Asphalt Roads, advanced schools & hospitals, electricity & parboiled water, shopping malls, children's playgrounds, and tourist areas) throughout the country, they refused to do so [probably an attempt to keep the majority in darkness so as not to compete with them] and by so doing they continued to hold citizenship to the U.S. (the nation they felt enslaved in.)

They also found it convenient to continue taking out Liberia's money to go to the hospital, go to school, buy expensive homes, and spend most of their vacations in the U.S.

Ummmmm! What is the purpose of having a country for yourselves if you knew you couldn't have made it conducive for your habitat? I must emphatically say that in terms of black's ability to achieve well for themselves without the white man's presence and pieces of advice, Liberia is the perfect example of what blacks can or can't do for themselves.

I take Liberia as a case study because it is the only black African country that did not experience colonial rule and, thus, was not raised or nurtured in any way by white people. The poor state of the black immigrant country at present (2018) is a direct result of what black judgment and lack of innovation have done to Africa, particularly Liberia. Once again, this was why I pondered so much about blackness.

What possible reasons did a US president hit at blacks?

So, when U.S. President [think] degraded Africans with such an opprobrious word like "shitholes," the questions become; why a fellow human being should reduce another human species to nothing with such description as "shitholes?" Why are we (black people) discriminated against by the white people?

So, while blacks may feel insulted and angered by all manner of debasement, I think they should exhale a little breath of patience and tolerance to explore any possible circumstance surrounding the issues to which anyone might inwardly be speaking. In so doing, we will ask ourselves other questions like: why do the white people have so much advantage over the black people? Are we responsible one way or the other for what is happening to us now? And, most importantly, what are we prepared to do about what is happening now?

The answer to the president's debasing of black people is a natural disparity created by the forces of the air that this book has been exploring.

But most African countries are developing

Figure 5: View of Ivory Coast, West Africa

But most Africans may argue that some countries like Kenya, Ivory Coast, Nigeria, and Ghana [excluding South Africa, where the white people still hold Ministerial posts] are developing.

To that, I want to say they are simply building on the brain work first laid down by their colonial powers [the white nations], which subjugated them before granting them half freedom. It is what they continue to do when you hear about development planning.

For example, the styles of city layout, house construction, and road construction that beautify Ivory Coast today with all the skyscrapers in this picture were the efforts of the white French colonizers who colonized the country before passing it over to the black indigenes on 7 August 1960. This is why I can say emphatically that the black Ivorian is simply thriving on the footprint of the white Ivorian who still lives in the country as a businessman.

Thus, the Ivory Coast looks like a European country, but that is because the French from Europe nurtured the people and established the system that has made the nation what it is today. The same can be attributed to all British colonies, like Nigeria, Ghana, and Kenya.

Hence, it's no shame to say that everything that black people have [The popular language to communicate in, the popular way to dress, the court system of marriage, the governing system, the church worship system, the road network system, the housing system, the lighting system, the water system, even the way to have a woman in bed, etc, etc] are all from the white world.

The only way I can see black people boasting of their knowledge is when they begin to invent new ideas and systems [definitely will have to build on top of any available system] to use to develop/advance Africa to put her in a position to compete with the rest of the world at some level similar to this book that brings new ideas from Africa to add to, modify and reinforce existing ideas in theology.

To this end, I want to congratulate a Liberian Scientist, Dr. Dougbeh Christopher Nyan, who invented a new technology while working in the US Food and Drug Administration (FDA).

Dr. Nyan and I hail from the Grebo tribe in Southeastern Liberia, and our hometowns share common boundaries. He is from Killeapo, and I am from Putuken (maternal) and Jarkaken (paternal).

Dr. Nyan's invention (Nyan Test) is a scientific breakthrough registered among scientific accomplishments in the world of medicines. Because of its simplicity of use, it has the potential to lift Africa to a new level.

This son of Liberia first came to the Western world in the late 1980s during the rule of the first native-born Liberian president, Samuel K. Doe. He went to Germany, where he studied human medicine, and later did his postdoctoral fellowship at the National Institute of Health, USA.

As anyone can understand, Dougbeh's exposure to Western equipment and methodology has helped him study to develop a rapid test that can detect and simultaneously differentiate at least three to seven infections at the same time within 10 to 40 minutes [bravo for not being complacent for every scientist one way or the other learned from another to bring forth his/her brain works.]

This report of new, quick-to-report-result equipment is said to be a diagnostic test that solves the clinical problem in most African countries, where the lack of sophisticated diagnostic devices and limited expertise in high-tech diagnostics exist.

His invention is a breakthrough in eliminating diagnostic problems that hinder the clinical decision-making ability of healthcare providers in most parts of Africa.

The report says his innovation is easy to use in any setting. The device is also said to detect and distinguish multiple infections with the same symptoms in patients with yellow fever, malaria, and Ebola.

His invention could be well above grade compared to

most [available] testing methods that take 3 – 7 days, whereas Dougbeh's device gives test results in 10 – 40 minutes.

He deserves credit for this high-quality level of innovation in the field of medicinal science.

Surprisingly [and for obvious reasons], the US Food and Drug Administration (FDA) removed his name from a scientific research paper and the development of a medical test after a successful work. Still, Dougbeh had to go through a stressful battle with the FDA by filing a complaint against the organization, and after a lengthy inquiry initiated by Congressman Lamar Smith, the US oversight committee on Science, Space, and Technology granted him the right to own the invention. So, in October 2016, the FDA returned the patent document to Nyan, a document awarded by the United States Patent and Trademark Office (USPTO.)

This son of Killeapo Town, a little town before my hometown, is en route from Monrovia to Harper City, Maryland County. He is currently working on the second prototype of his innovation after obtaining positive results from his first prototype.

The results have been verified with human clinical samples and published in several respected scientific journals, such as Nature-Scientific Reports.

His innovation has the potential to be a game changer on the continent in the detection and management of infectious diseases, which is essential for quality patient care.

Dr. Nyan's invention has just been confirmed in one of the News from Space given to me to broadcast about black man's time to receive science of invention. To this, I'm proud to say wake up Africa- for more science is yet to come, but this [possibly] may not mature enough should Africans remain impatient towards trials and errors [it's a situation in which scientists {even writers and singers} find themselves when they do things (create, write and sing). They make mistakes but keep doing the same thing repeatedly by adding and subtracting until it gets better.]

Now hear this: The reason people of great knowledge make mistakes [even without knowing why] is due to spiritual interferences wherein one force decides to teach something, but another force is trying to stop it, which brings about wavering (shaking) of the mind [Mind - is a receptacle in the brain that receives impulses {landings and departures of forces} from the air and the heart].

Now close your eyes and visualize stilt water [sitting so calmly]; suddenly, something jumps into it. What do you see? Undoubtedly, the water shakes and divides into waves running in different directions or even splashing into the air before recollecting again. When this happens, something is disturbed; the fishes [inhabitants of the water] may run away from their positions and may take time to gather again.

So, when we make mistakes while we feel the urge to do something, our brain is shattered. Still, we don't need to give up on it even if it means we may fail since our persistence brings out the best results we desire [so, it is written in the holy Bible that one should "Pray {call/invite/invoke the spirit} without ceasing"].

EXTRAS

Although many theologians usually downplay the truth about how the Bible didn't say everything mankind needs to know about God. They refuse to acknowledge publicly that the Bible contains human errors [not God's errors]. The theocratic ministry of the Lord Jesus Christ, brought to earth by God in December 2005, is responsible for unveiling these truths. This section of this book contains a few of them as extras, among other things. Since all these things cannot be written at once, the ministry would publish any remaining things in tracts from time to time.

Where did the rich and the poor come from?

Often, [by my hearing], some people regret having been born into poverty, and they say when they die and have the opportunity to come back, they shall not go to poor parents again. For black Africans and [perhaps] other races, they say they shall be born into the white race because they think the white race is superior and rich.

But who has ever chosen where to be born? Who was there when he/she was manufactured into a human being?

Obviously, no one has control over that. In fact, God did not make any man poor; neither did he make any man rich.

God hears all these accusations against Him, so He sent me to clarify what is happening in the world.

He says He made all men equal. He provided everything [the resources of the earth] free for all. He [having come down as Jesus] taught the people [his disciples] how to do things in the world. He exemplified to them how to live together, abandon owning property, abandon chasing after the world's riches, share, and work together to enjoy all. So, that was socialism and communism/communality.

God says Satan is the architect of the order of this world today. Satan is the one using the divide-and-rule system by introducing an ownership system into the world of human beings. Yet, he (Satan) makes some rich [in fact, those with hard hearts are easy to work with]. At the same time, he suffers most of the people who, for some reason, waver all the time, making it harder for him (Satan) to work consistently with them. For some, it is due to the sins of their ancestors who may have failed their duties to appease Him (Satan) at some point in time, yet for some, poverty is Satan's way of punishing them for some reasons he knows, opposite to the way God uses His Grace [discretion] to save some people out of specific sins.

How this happens is that Satan, through His demons (the ancestral spirits of each family line), is in the habit of denying other people the abundance of things of this world through several means that take away money or, in the pre-money era, was unproductivity. In this money era, He breeds sicknesses into families, He breeds troubles, He breeds bad habits like drunkenness or smoking or extreme sexual desires, all of which drain out money and at the same time land people into trouble.

He even breeds instability of the mind so that people get weary of doing certain things that they think would bring them more money. As they keep on changing from one thing to another, they also get caught up in other unfavorable conditions, so they continue to be down. Thus, instability [shifting and shifting] is a general condition that the largest population of the world suffers from so that they keep away from achieving wealth/more money. Those who achieve wealth in this world know this phenomenon. They don't waver; instead, they are persistent.

Therefore, you men, stop accusing God of disparities that you find among

yourselves. He is fair in all things.

What Convicts Me to Write These Things

When I started receiving the voices of Christ's messengers, I first doubted what I was hearing. I asked them questions and refused to write down the things, but they kept telling me, "Write down what you are hearing, for you shall approve them yourself." They told me that I needed not to worry so much because everything was written in the Bible long before I was born, and all I could do was to search the scriptures, and I would find the truth.

The messengers brought me messages one after another and told me Satan's time is out now; we are heading to judgment time, and people need to know how God is going to render His judgment when the hour reaches. He will judge Satan. He will judge the church. He will judge nations, and He will judge people. [Judgment of the church and the nations begins with the rulers of the churches and the nations.]

So, from 2006 to mid–2008, I was under the Spirit, seeing visions and hearing voices as I walked, sat down, or lay down.

I was given many physical examples to learn how the Spirit enables man to walk, lie down, yawn, cough, sneeze, cry, etc.

A demo was also performed on me to know how a man obtains sexual erection. I also learned the power of speaking Spiritual languages (tongues) and making music. Similarly, I received the power of healing and prophesying [Just for training purposes]. See under EXTRAS at the end of this book.

Why Did I Receive Many Gifts?

The powers of tongue speaking, singing, healing, and prophesying were special gifts I received to learn and look behind the prophets of all ages and to know how the gift of singing is given to people who make music.

These gifts were given to me to assure myself of what the prophets do. For example, one of my eldest sisters was so surprised when I revealed to her the name of a particular guy who was in the habit of entering her room every afternoon to harass her for lovemaking only whenever everybody had left the house.

This happened one afternoon when suddenly the spirit descended on me and told me to get up and go to my paternal brother's house, about 20-minute high-pace walking distance. This wasn't the first time I was told to go somewhere without reason, only to get there before knowing why.

So, I went to my brother's house, where I met only my paternal sister [she and my brother share a single mother].

So, as soon as I entered her room, the spirit descended back on me, putting words on my tongue and saying to my sister, "You were lucky this afternoon that he didn't rape you, but if you continue to let him into your room, he shall rape you one day." Upon saying this, my sister was shocked but admitted exactly that a guy almost raped her a few minutes ago before I got there. She asked me how I got to know everything that I said about the attempted rape of her, and I answered that the spirit had revealed that to me. I told her that the spirit commanded me to come to their house without letting me know what I was coming for, not until I arrived at her place.

Therefore, my sister erased the notion of my insanity from her mind. She was not anymore with those who labeled me to be insane. Obviously, everyone said that I was insane since they didn't understand that I was going through Spiritual training that made me say or do some strange things and behave weirdly all the time.

This is to mention one of the things about the prophets I was taught so that I could look behind their powers and tell them that everything I say about them is true.

The above physical examples performed on me served as the first approval that I got to believe that something real was taking place.

The second thing that strengthened me more was when the Spirit told me to search the book of Ezekiel 28 Chapter. No verse was given. So, I began to search Chapter 28 of the book, and when I reached verse 13, I felt something choking me to have a break. Then I continued through 14, 15, & 16, but as soon as I finished verse 17, I heard a voice clearly saying, "Stop, that's it!!!" The verses of focus are 28:13 & 17, which say that Satan was in the Garden of Eden and was thrown down to the earth when pride entered Him.

This was a true confirmation of the voice that said to me that the Garden is not on this earth but is still in heaven.

Ezekiel 28:13 - 17) Thou has been in ***Eden the Garden of God;*** *every precious stone was thy covering, the sardius, topaz, and the diamond, the beryl, the onyx, and the jasper, the sapphire, the emerald, and the carbuncle, and gold: the* ***workmanship*** *of thy tabrets and of thy pipes was prepared in thee in the day that thou was created.*

:14) Thou art the anointed cherub that covereth; and have set thee so: Thou wast upon the holy mountain of God; thou hast walked up and down in the midst of the stones of fire.

:15) Thou wast perfect in thy ways from the day that thou wast created, till iniquity was found in thee.

:16) By the multitude of thy merchandise they have filled the midst of thee with violence, and thou hast sinned: therefore I will cast thee as profane out of the mountain of God: and I will destroy thee, O covering cherub, from the midst of the stones of fire.

:17) Thine heart was lifted up because of thy beauty, thou hast corrupted thy wisdom by reason of thy brightness: I will ***cast thee to the ground****, I will lay thee before Kings, that they may behold thee.*

*(This is KJV, but the NIV says, "****So I threw you to the earth.****")*

Why must our world go through the same as the old world?

A Go-Over Storytelling

The Bible tells a story about the end of the first world, marked by Noah's building of an Ark/Boat, and the beginning of a new world, marked by the end of the Flood.

A spirit retold this story to me like a replay of a recorded disk. It was told in detail more than is written in the Bible.

The story encompasses the entire human creation, beginning with Adam and Eve and ending with Noah out of the boat. And when all was told, the spirit told me that everything that I needed to know to confirm the authenticity of what was replayed to me was already written by many prophets who came before me. Hence, all I needed to do was to read the Bible and other books of other prophets. So, over the years until 2019, I have been coming across a lot of information, and among them is the story from the book of the Latter Days Saints Church about where we came from.

Well, I came to the US on a visitor's visa, so I had to go

through a process to get a work permit that would allow me to find a job that would help me raise money to publish the books that God has inspired me to write. So, while waiting for it, on Sunday morning, May 5, 2019, at 7:10 AM, I came across the topic "Where did I come from?" in a teaching Tract of the Latter-day Saints (LDS) Church. I was studying with them every week, so I got the pamphlet.

The topic "Where did I come from? is on page 2 of the Tract (pamphlet) titled "The Plan of Salvation." That pamphlet is written therein, "Your life didn't begin at birth, nor will it end at death. You are made up of a spirit body (sometimes called the soul) and a physical body. Your Heavenly Father created your spirit, and you lived with Him as a spirit before you were born on earth. You knew and loved Him, and He knew and loved you. This period is called pre-earth life".

No church I've heard of has this teaching, except the Latter-day Saints. I'm grateful I met them.

NOW THIS IS THE STORY OF THE CREATION OF PHYSICAL MAN: The spirit of God that brought the details of what you've just read from the Latter Days' book of man's history told me that man's life began in the Garden of Eden as a spirit, and he (Man) existed in that Spirit world for so many centuries, reproducing children that expanded over many generations before he culminated into a physical being like we are today.

In God's allegory [using a symbol to represent something else] of telling this old-world story to Moses, He (God) revealed the names and places of these spiritual generations and their Kingdoms in a way that seemed like they existed physically because some of the names and places already existed in the physical.

This is one reason why this physical world must experience all the stages and happenings that the Spiritual man and his generations went through. It is bound [Must] for them to experience everything before the end comes for the physical man, too.

Mysteries in the Book of Revelation

True, the Bible cautions Christians about falsehoods from many people who profess the name of Christ, but the same Bible says the Church should examine them.

This doubting and examining of people once took place among the believers when Paul had his encounter with Jesus "on his way to Damascus." The believers doubted him, but they had to examine him for a long time to believe that he had received the Spirit and the Light from Christ, and afterward, they believed.

These things happen because of the mysteries in God's doings that are far beyond man's understanding, no matter how much he (man) has studied the word of God because that's what He is—the mystery God.

Therefore, for those who believe that during plenty falsehoods, God is still not speaking today, we want to say to them that they are still looking for understanding in several passages of the same book of the Bible. One such passage is Revelation 4:6-9, which exposes us to another allegory: ([6] Also in front of the throne there was what looked like a sea of glass, clear as crystal. In the center, around the throne, were four living creatures, and they were covered with eyes, in front and in back. [7] The first living creature was like a lion, the second was like an ox, the third had a face like a man, the fourth was like a flying eagle. [8] Each of the four living creatures had six wings and was covered with eyes all around, even under its wings. Day and night they never stop saying:

"'Holy, holy, holy
is the Lord God Almighty,'
who was, and is, and is to come."

Whenever the living creatures give glory, honor and thanks to him who sits on the throne and who lives forever and ever.

The Bible says they're "Creatures", there is a meaning to that.

One was "Like a lion." I (PAUL) shall demonstrate to the world in a physical manner how that "lion-like" creature has manifested unto me. One "Had a face like a man," I shall prove that "Man like" face. One was "Like a flying eagle." this "Flying like eagle" behavior is one that I experience and shall be demonstrated publicly when I have had the opportunity to do so. Another was "Like an ox," which I also experienced while alone.

These spiritual forces (angels) manifest today, but no one knows that.

ABOUT MOSES - THE WRITER OF GENESIS

Moses was a real man born of a woman through sexual intercourse, but he was something else that made the King stupid in his own wisdom that was meant to stop God from doing what was planned in the Spirit realm before the birth of the young Moses.

King Pharaoh of Egypt wanted to kill all the boy children of the Hebrews not only because they were getting plenty but mainly because the gods & goddesses of Egypt had known that a child was born of the Spirit that would cause trouble in the land of Egypt.

These gods and goddesses tormented the King and his cabinets so much so that they couldn't find peace unless they killed the Hebrews boys since God hid the child Moses from them [the gods and goddesses couldn't identify Moses among the babies, so they chose to kill all].

But not even the gods & goddesses have the power to

stop God's manifestations. So, God used Pharaoh's daughter to save the life of the wanted king of the Hebrews in Egypt. Then God smuggled the Hebrew child into the same palace where the decree was issued to kill him.

She took the young baby Moses to the very Palace of the King, yet the king did nothing. He accepted the Hebrew child as his stepson.

The million-dollar question is, why didn't he kill this one of the Hebrews? **Is this not the wisdom of God and the stupidity of man?**

Moses was already ordained in the Spirit for this mission, which led him out of Egypt when the right time came. He did not even know what was happening to him, so he told God, "I am not worthy to stand in front of Pharaoh." But he had to go with the power he received while on Mount Sinai.

This book, now segmented as 'Genesis—God's Architectural Work,' was written by a man named Moses. Unfortunately for his people, he did not explain it due to the tough time they gave him for food and drink in the wilderness. As a result, this book has caused a lot of confusion among mankind and made the scripture difficult to understand.

Now, seeing the many arguments among the churches as the world approaches its end, God does not want to remain silent on this matter, so He re-established Himself in this world for a look back into creation. Therefore, this book comes from the background of telling you all about these mysteries that took place long ago. It also intends to strengthen believers that God is still with us and His word is true.

So, let those who have ears hear, for God needs no excuse from anyone. No one shall say, 'I did not know it so.' This is why God has to tell His story again.

Latter Days Saints church has a purpose

Thank God when I encountered the Latter-day Saints on April 11th, 2019. Two young men from the church (also called "Mormons") working as missionaries for the Lord Jesus knocked on my door one afternoon to share with me the word of God from His son Jesus Christ to other ancient prophets.

The visit of these two young guys, Elder Boam and Elder Hints ["Elder" is the title for all teachers in the Mormon church], revealed to me the news about a fourteen year old young white American named "Joseph Smith" to whom [it is said] the Lord Jesus sent a messenger [said to be a man named "Moroni" who first lived among the ancient inhabitants of the Americas and died after burying some information written on Gold Plates left in his care by his father named "Mormon"].

Listen to what Joseph Smith said in the introduction of the Book of Mormon, and I quote, "Then a glorified, resurrected being appeared to the prophet Joseph Smith and instructed him relative to the ancient record and its destined translation into the English language," unquote.

Well, this act of a spirit appearing [as a messenger] in the name of someone who died long ago was clarified to me back in 2008. For more on this, check under EXTRAS in my other title, Interpretation First.

Smith then followed the instructions and unveiled the Gold Plates in 1823, which Moroni had previously hidden in the "Hill Cumorah" in Manchester, New York, U.S.A.

To me, Smith's description of the origin of these plates seems to point at some ancient Israelis [He called them "Lamanites"] who migrated to the continent and settled among the ancestors of the American Indians several hundred years before he (Smith) was born.

Also, by reading 3 Nephi chapter 11 [Mormon's book] about Jesus' appearance to grant authority to him (Nephi) to baptize people in his (Jesus') name [Mormon page 327], it appears to me that Nephi and the other prophets in the book of Mormon were not Jews and could have been left out of Jewish history books of reporting the things of the Lord Jesus Christ.

Their written accounts [Smith said] include some of the things that appear in the Holy Bible [Genesis 11:1-9], telling how the whole world had one language at first until the people chose to build a tower to reach the heavens. God confused them, and they scattered all over the earth into different languages.

Remember, I have offered an expanded version of the Babel story.

The information contained in the plates was combined with the story of Smith's encounter with the messenger [the spirit that appeared to him in the name of Moroni] and the statements of others he (Smith) called "Witnesses" to constitute what is now called "The Book of Mormon," which is used by the Church of Mormon as a complementary study book to the Holy Bible.

So, why does the Latter Days Saints (Mormon) church matter to me? It matters to me because God confirmed to me that Joseph Smith represents God's Spirit's choosing of the White race [in the US] after starting with the semi-white race of humankind [in Ur, Middle East].

So, after the same God has chosen me [from Liberia, West Africa] from the black race, He said this brings an end to Christ's visit to all Races-semi-white, white, and black, to show every humankind that He had made them all, and they're all equal before Him, and He came to them all.

Finally, God is in Africa

So, in January 2006, the black man eventually took his place, and I, PAUL ["PAUL means Prophet Appointed Unto the Lord"], was elected qualified since I have been arguing and yearning for the truth on two major issues: Why is the black man alone trailing [backward] behind all races, and why are all the churches divided and arguing among themselves about the one Bible that they say one God had inspired?

Apart from these two questions come another: Why

black man doesn't have technology but depends on the white man alone?

In response to my daring inquisitions, the Lord Almighty sent His spirit upon me [in a way that is so weird] that has culminated into four major books that answer God's Three R's; (1) R-Review the teachings the people have done, (2) R-Reveal details of judgment to come in Heaven, and (3) R-Make Right for sinners [all of us] to make ourselves right before the end comes.

My restless soul triggered the truth

So, I received these understandings because the Highest Spirit had seen me ponder the uniqueness of the Bible coupled with the things I saw wrong about black men in a quest to understand why the black man is so different from all other human races that he (black man) always depends on the help of the other peoples of the world.

The word "WHY" was too much in my head. I began to explore all the things we know about black people and Africa as a whole, and I also began to compare and contrast them all, particularly beginning in 1999, at age 33, when I first went to study how to use a computer.

My first month learning how to use a computer was fascinating when the 3.5 Windows 97 could talk back to me each time I booted it. A Desktop computer with a name like "Hemien" would display on the screen, saying, "Hemien is checking memory." Whenever I touched a wrong key, the computer prompted me with the word "Error." It startled me each time the computer communicated with me to guide me to do the right thing that needed to be done. Oh my God, that was so fascinating to me.

This type of communication from a machine, not a human being, made me wonder how the white man has advanced his magical powers from darkness (unseen) to light (seen).

Due to my fascination, a sort of attraction to technology, and I still do, I would say to myself, "Why wasn't I born unto the white race? Why am I not in the white man's country to study technology?" This also brought another question to my mind, such as, "What is so wrong with this black race that it hasn't been able to participate in technology?"

To answer these questions, I said to myself that we need to examine races and compare the other six continents to Africa in order to see our lifestyles, developments, and ingenuities.

Those who contributed to this book

My gratitude goes to Apostle Abraham Joe Kiamue and his four-man Committee members of the *Church of God Christian Ministry*, Monrovia, Liberia, West Africa. Thank you for believing in the Theocratic Ministry's work and dedicating your time to providing your reviews and comments for this book.

Also, thank you for accepting the role of a working partner to collaborate with the Theocratic ministry in recruiting its first team of entertainers who will help exalt our Lord Jesus through songs of praise while accompanying the Storyteller whenever he goes out on God's mission.

Committee's Commentary on the Interpretation Second

(Original copy edited but the content remains same)

After carefully reviewing Interpretation Second, we found it quite interesting that this book is inspiring. In particular, in part one, we discovered many new things that were not taught in the Bible school we attended in the past.

However, part one of this book is actually about theology (the study of God). This part of the book goes deeper into Genesis with descriptions placed place by place.

This book, Interpretation Second, is an eye-opening read for the religious community and the world at large.

The writer of this book, Mr. Paul Tarsleh, has brought light to what was hidden. God's servant (Paul) clearly revealed Noah's Ark, which Noah built under God's instruction, in terms of its spiritual and physical stories.

We recommend this book not just to the religious community but to the world, too, as it will open everyone's eyes to what was hidden and is now revealed in it.

Please meet these noble men and women of God.

1. **Apostle Abraham Joe Kiamue**

Apostle Kiamue, founder/general overseer of the Church of God Christian Ministry, born June 20, 1988, holds an AA degree in theology and several other diplomas and certificates in Biblical Studies.

2. **Pastor P. Eric Mandeh**

Pastor Eric, resident pastor and founding pastor of the Church of God Christian Ministry, was born on May 20, 1998, a high school graduate and obtained a "C" certificate in education.

3. **Min. Ophelia M. Vonyeegar**

Min. Ophelia, a choir director's assistant at the Church of God Christian Ministry, was born on March 18, 1990, and is a college dropout.

4. **Sis. Keturah Nahn**

Sis. Keturah Nahn was born on October 9, 1993, and obtained an AA degree in education and many other certificates in biblical studies. She is the children's ministry teacher at the Church of God Christian Ministry.

5. **Min. Annie Payway**

Min. Annie Payway, choir director and head at the Church of God Christian Ministry, was born on March 24, 2004, and is still in high school.

About the author, PAUL

The name 'Paul' should actually be spelled all cap like "PAUL" as each letter stands for *'P'="Principal, 'A'= "Agent", 'U'= "United", to the 'L'= "Lord" Jesus.*

PAUL *Tarsleh* was born unto the union of *Jonah Seah Tarsleh* and *Elizabeth T. Jah* in Liberia - West Africa. He is married and is a father of seven (7) children.

His father was assassinated by a gunshot when he was yet six years old. He was reared by his grandparents and had difficulties getting money to attend school.

He graduated from high school in 1989 and came top of his class, so he earned a government scholarship to attend the University of Liberia. He intended to study Mass Communication and Politics there, but all this failed for him due to the country's civil war, which broke out in December of that year and lasted for 13 years.

While in school, he became a student journalist. After graduation, he started working with two newspapers, Business Digest and Sports Chronicle, which were owned and managed by one person. Later, the business paper turned political and became *Liberian Digest*, while the sports paper closed due to the war.

After a few months, the political paper was closed in 1990, and he had to flee the nation's capital to find himself in exile in the nearest bordering country, Ivory Coast.

In the Ivory Coast, he became a refugee mining gold to provide for his family's basic needs. With this refugee status, all his dreams were shattered.

In 1999, he moved to the central city (Tabou), where he took advantage of a United Nations-funded vocational school. There, he earned an 18-month bookkeeping certificate, the highest level of education he has to date.

Despite his misfortune in pursuing a degree in journalism, he has not left the writing world.

In the two and a half years from 2006 to mid–2008, his interest in writing was enhanced by the mysterious voice that gave him stories to write to provide answers to various issues dangling on the minds of people, including religious communities.

This book is the result of what he learned from that mysterious voice.

Before this mysterious voice, Paul was a churchgoer with a general secretary position in the Effort Baptist Church in Tabou, a Refugee community.

PAUL also held various jobs in the secular world. Below are some of his job profiles.

***Africa (excluding his pre-war jobs):**

- Foreman at European Union (EU) Swamp Development (2001).
- Grades 5-7 English Teacher at Tabou-Bilangual Education Center (T-BEC) (2002).
- Small Business Management Instructor at Tabou-Technical Education Center (T-TEC) (2005).
- Youth President for the Liberian Refugee Youth in Tabou, Ivory Coast (2005).
- Project Head for the World Food Program (WFP) Food For Work Project for Road Maintenance in Tabou, Ivory Coast (2005).
- Bookkeeper at Messiah Mission Institute, Monrovia, Liberia (mid-2008).
- Grades 7-9 English Teacher at Messiah Mission Institute, Monrovia, Liberia (mid-2008).
- Bookkeeper for Cuttington University Credit Union, Gbarnga, Bong County, Liberia (2009-2010).
- Bookkeeper at Hotel Serenghetti, Restaurant & Bar in Gbarnga, Bong County (mid-2010).
- Procurement Officer at ArcelorMittal-Liberia, Buchanan, Grand Bassa County, Liberia (December. 2010 to August. 2014).

***USA:**

- Variety of short-term jobs (2015 to 2017) (Warehouse jobs, Packaging jobs, Printing job, etc.)
- Direct Support Professional in the Human Service sector, providing developmental support for individuals with disabilities (2017 to the time of publishing this book-2024).

Finding himself in the human service sector as a Direct Support Professional, he sees God preparing him for the Theocratic Ministry's future responsibility to take care of the people of the disability community.

www.ingramcontent.com/pod-product-compliance
Lightning Source LLC
LaVergne TN
LVHW041145150826
845673LV00001B/66

* 9 7 9 8 8 9 5 6 9 7 1 5 3 *